Building
Envelopes

Architecture Briefs is a Princeton Architectural Press series designed to address a variety of single topics of interest to architecture students and young professionals. Field-specific and technical information, ranging from hand-drawn to digital methods, are presented in a user-friendly manner alongside basics of architectural thought, design, and construction. The series familiarizes readers with the concepts and skills necessary to successfully translate ideas into built form.

Also in this series:

Architects Draw, Sue Ferguson Gussow

Digital Fabrications, Lisa Iwamoto

Architecture Briefs
The Foundations of Architecture

Building Envelopes: An Integrated Approach

Jenny Lovell

Princeton Architectural Press
New York

Published by
Princeton Architectural Press
37 East Seventh Street
New York, New York 10003

For a free catalog of books, call 1.800.722.6657.
Visit our website at www.papress.com.

© 2010 Princeton Architectural Press
All rights reserved
Printed and bound in China
13 12 11 10 4 3 2 1 First edition

No part of this book may be used or reproduced in any manner without written permission from the publisher, except in the context of reviews.

Every reasonable attempt has been made to identify owners of copyright. Errors or omissions will be corrected in subsequent editions.

Editor: Becca Casbon
Designer: Jan Haux

Special thanks to: Nettie Aljian, Bree Anne Apperley, Sara Bader, Nicola Bednarek, Janet Behning, Carina Cha, Tom Cho, Penny (Yuen Pik) Chu, Carolyn Deuschle, Russell Fernandez, Pete Fitzpatrick, Wendy Fuller, Clare Jacobson, Linda Lee, Laurie Manfra, John Myers, Katharine Myers, Steve Royal, Dan Simon, Andrew Stepanian, Jennifer Thompson, Paul Wagner, Joseph Weston, and Deb Wood of Princeton Architectural Press
—Kevin C. Lippert, publisher

Library of Congress Cataloging-in-Publication Data
Lovell, Jenny, 1967–
Building envelopes : an integrated approach / Jenny Lovell. – 1st ed.
p. cm. – (Architecture brief)
Includes bibliographical references.
ISBN 978-1-56898-818-4 (alk. paper)
1. Facades—Design and construction. I. Title.
TH2235.L68 2010
729'.1–dc22

2009040572

Dedication

Time belongs to everyone.
 —P. W. F, 3 years old

I'm putting this story in your mouth so that you can tell someone else.
 —L. G. F, 3 years old

Image credits:

All images are the author's unless otherwise indicated. Images marked with an * indicate figures remixed by the author with kind permission of the original creator.

13(2): Matt Herman (Buro Happold)
18(2), 32(1), 44(1), 45(2-3), 46(4-6), 47(7-9), 48(10), 51(2): Buro Happold
19(3): Jodi Jacobson (www.istockphoto.com)
19(4): Samuel Kessler (www.istockphoto.com)
19(5): Melissa King (www.istockphoto.com)
19(6): Declan McCullagh (www.mccullagh.org)
19(7): Phat Trance
21(14): Laurie Knight (www.istockphoto.com)
22(1): Teresa Hohn
23(2)*: Nikken Sekkei, Japan
25(3)*: http://koeppen-geiger.vu-wien.ac.at
28(5), 29(6): Jen Cayton (produced in Autodesk Ecotect)
29(7), 132(1), 133(2-3), 134(4), 135(6-8), 136(9-10), 137(11-14), 138(15), 139(16): SHoP Architects (www.shoparc.com)
33(2), 34(3), 66(11), 71(9-10), 76(5), 82(10-12), 95(4-5): Center for Architecture Science and Ecology (CASE), Rensselaer Polytechnic Institute (www.case.rpi.edu)
38(5)*: John Fernandez, Associate Professor, MIT
39(6-9), 79(2-5), 100(3-4), 101(5-7), 104(10-13), 105(16), 106(17), 107(18-19), 108(20): Allford Hall Monaghan Morris (www.ahmm.co.uk)
41(14): Richard Cooper
41(15): Rod Dorling
42(16-18): Alicia Pivaro
49(3)*: Stewart Brand, *How Buildings Learn, What Happens After They're Built* (New York: Viking Penguin, 1994)
51(3)*: Tim Cooke (Cannon Design)
62(1), 63(4-5): Jan Bitter (www.janbitter.de)
63(6): Sauerbruch Hutton (www.sauerbruchhutton.de)
64(8), 65(9-10), 85(4): Annette Kisling
68(3)*: Professor Paul J. Donnelly, Sam Fox School of Design and Visual Arts, Graduate School of Architecture and Urban Design, Washington University in St. Louis and Richard Janis of TAO and Associates, Inc.
81(8), 140(1), 142(3-4), 143(5-6), 144(7-8), 145(9), 146(10-11), 147(12): Lifschutz Davidson (www.lifschutzdavidson.com)
85(3): Sauerbruch Hutton and Lepkowski Studios, Berlin
87(6-7): Hoberman Associates (www.hoberman.com)
88(8): Foster + Partners
92(1)*: McKinsey & Company
94(2-3): Dr. Raymond Cole, from Cole, R.J., Robinson, J.R., Brown, Z., and O'Shea, M., "Re-Contextualising the Notion of Comfort," *Journal of Building Research & Information* 36, no. 4 (2008)

98(1), 99(2), 102(8), 103(9), 105(14-15), 109(21-22): Timothy Soar (www.soarportfolio.co.uk)
110(1), 111(2-3), 112(5), 113(4, 6-8), 114(9), 115(12): Arup Associates (www.arupassociates.com)
112(4), 114(10): Paul Brislin (Arup Associates)
114(11): Filippo Cefis (Arup Associates)
115(13): Eeling See (Arup Associates)
116(1), 122(14): Allies and Morrison (www.alliesandmorrison.co.uk)
117(2, 4-5), 118(6-7), 122(15), 123(16-17): Dennis Gilbert, VIEW (www.viewpictures.co.uk)
121(13)*: Energy Consumption Guide 54: Energy Efficiency in Further & Higher Education, table 2, 7. (Watford: BRECSU)
125(1), 128(8), 131(11-12): Tim Crocker (www.timcrocker.co.uk)
126(2), 127(3-6), 128(7), 129(9-10): Hawkins\Brown (www.hawkinsbrown.co.uk)
134(5): Paperfarm
141(2): Smoothe International Ltd

Table of Contents

- 8 Foreword
- 10 Acknowledgments
- 12 Introduction

Section I:
- 16 **Feedback Loops of Form and Performance**
- 18 Comfort at the Scale of the Body
- 22 Climate and Context
- 30 Interdisciplinary to Transdisciplinary
- 36 Materials and Fabrication
- 42 Building Simulation Tools
- 49 Life Cycle Analysis

Section II:
- 54 **Elements of a Holistic Approach**
- 60 Air: Flow and Ventilation
- 67 Heat: Gain and Loss
- 72 Water: Systems and Collection
- 77 Materials: Assemblies and Installation
- 83 Daylighting: Comfort and Control
- 89 Energy: Minimizing and Maximizing

Section III:
- 96 **Integrated Building Envelope Strategies**
- 98 Live/Work: Adelaide Wharf Housing and 160 Tooley Street Offices
- 110 Deep Plan: Harlequin 1, BSkyB Transmission and Recording Facility
- 116 Feedback Loops: Faculty of English and Institute of Criminology
- 124 Plug-ins: Tooley Street Terrace
- 132 Maximizing Value: 290 Mulberry Street
- 140 Made to Measure: The Charlotte Building Offices

- 148 Notes
- 150 Bibliography
- 152 Case Study Project Credits

Foreword

The last century saw a radical change in the nature of the building envelope. Rather than being considered as part of the structure—a single, homogeneous plane perforated by openings—it began to be conceived instead as a separate layer that, relieved of any structural responsibility, could fulfill the sole function of protecting the interior of the building from the vagaries of the outside world.

At first sight, this separation of a building's structure from its envelope might be expected to be liberating, freeing the contemporary architect to invent new and radical solutions to the problems of creating building enclosure. But the reality, as this book makes clear, is at once more complex and more interesting. The design of the building envelope has to address a wide spectrum of issues, ranging from the technical performance of the individual materials and the nature of their assembly to the visual appearance and propriety of the resulting building form.

In setting down and explaining these various issues in this book, Jenny Lovell draws them fully into the design process, offering the prospect of generating architectural form and meaning directly from their resolution. For this to happen, an approach is required that fuses practical considerations of how a building works—how it maintains the physical comfort of its occupants—with aesthetic, or cultural, considerations of how a building looks—how it is assimilated into its context and what it represents. "Poetic sensibility integrated with pragmatic application," as Lovell describes it.

When addressing these issues in the past, an architect would, conventionally, have interpreted his obligations as being on the one hand to the client—for whom the building was being provided—and, on the other, to his own professional reputation. Today, however, this is no longer enough. The threat of climate change, and the growing recognition of the need to combat it, has given architects a fundamental obligation to design buildings that consume a minimum amount of resources in their production as well as in their long-term operation and maintenance.

Inventiveness and ingenuity are therefore critical to the design of building envelopes in the future, and the complete integration of the skills and experiences of all members of the design team will be fundamental to this process. The innovation needed is of a particular kind: it is not introduced in order to make one building look different from another, but is aimed at the development of new models and archetypes that have widespread relevance and application.

This requires a more thorough understanding of the issues that are to be addressed, more active research into the solutions that might be adopted, and more imaginative speculations as to how these problems might be solved. Because of the nature of the discipline, it also means architects must be capable of explaining these issues to their clients, thereby eliciting their support for the inevitable additional investment that will be required.

What this book also advocates, however, is that the architect should engage with the particularities of his or her specific project—the exact nature of the climate that it has to moderate, the precise types of activity it has to accommodate, and the context to which it has to contribute—to develop buildings of originality and imagination, buildings that go beyond the adoption of the run-of-the-mill solution.

A building's envelope forms the critical interface between its interior life and the environment of the external world. Its design is therefore at the heart of the architectural process, a process that will be both informed and stimulated by the guidance that this book provides.

Bob Allies
Allies and Morrison, London

Acknowledgments

Building Envelopes has been my first publishing venture, and as an architect I can now say that making a book is like designing a building, in that it truly takes a team to get it done. This book would not have been possible without a team of contributors that I would like to acknowledge as fully as I can.

Thank you to Jennifer Thompson at Princeton Architectural Press for having the interest and confidence in what I was saying to approach me to write this book in the first place and for initiating the process, to Clare Jacobson for her follow-through, and to my editor, Becca Casbon, and the rest of the team who truly realized this production.

Thank you to all my colleagues here at Washington University in St. Louis who enabled me to hit the ground running in 2008; to Dean Carmon Colangelo and the Sam Fox School Faculty Creative Activity Research Grant Committee for awarding me a grant that made this work possible; and to Dean Bruce Lindsey for his constant support, phenomenal knowledge, and the generous donation of his time. An enormous thank you goes to my research assistants: Jen Cayton (Wash. U. class of 2008), for her tireless dedication, calmness, and professionalism; and to Ekta Desai (Wash. U. class of 2010), who committed so many of my diagrams to digital format and who shared the delights and trials of Adobe Illustrator, always with good humor. Thank you to all my colleagues here in the Graduate School of Architecture and Urban Design, especially: Paul J. Donnelly, Robert McCarter, Peter MacKeith, and Michael Repovich for all of their feedback; and to the Sam Fox IT team of Richard, Bob, and Geoff, for the "megabytes." Thank you also to my former colleagues at the University of Virginia, who supported the very early stages of my book proposal: Julie Bargmann, Bill Sherman, Anselmo Canfora, and especially to my mentor, friend, and constant line of positive energy, William Morrish.

Thank you to those practices and people whose work is included in the book and who have contributed to it so very generously: Paul Monaghan, Simon Allford,

Morag Tait, Gemma Hall, and Lucy Swift at Allford Hall Monaghan Morris; Bob Allies, Graham Morrison, Jo Bacon, and Nicholas Champkins at Allies and Morrison; Declan O'Carroll, Paul Brizlin, Michael Beaven, and Eeling See at Arup Associates; Fiona Cousins, Tali Mejicovsky, and Andrew Hall at Arup; Patrick Bellew at Atelier Ten; Stewart Brand; Matt Herman and Ian Maddocks at Buro Happold; Tim Cooke at Cannon Design; Anna Dyson, Jason Vollen, EmilyRae Brayton, and Keith Van de Riet at CASE/Rensselaer; Dr. Raymond Cole at the University of British Columbia School of Architecture; Michael Cracknell and Stephen Mudie at Davis Langdon; Helen Newman and Nicola Hopwood at Glenn Howells Architects; David Bickle and Jessica Billam at Hawkins\Brown; Chuck Hoberman and Craig Holland at Hoberman Associates; Michelle Pinkston at HOK St. Louis; James Miles at Lifschutz Davidson Sandilands; Terry Willis, Per-Anders Enkvist, and Monica Runggatscher at McKinsey & Company; Associate Professor John Fernandez at MIT; Roberto Bicchiarelli at Permasteelisa Group; Louisa Hutton, Lina Lahiri, and Isabelle Hartmann at Sauerbruch Hutton; Gregg Pasquarelli, Tiffany Taraska, Nadine Berger, and Corie Sharples at SHoP Architects; Assistant Professor Herman Pontzer at the Washington University in St. Louis Department of Anthropology; Jesse Fahnestock at Vattenfall AB; and Mark Rylander, Martha Bohm, Kira Gould, and Kevin Burke at William McDonough + Partners.

Thank you for all the conversations I have had with students, faculty, practitioners, and specialists—may they be ongoing!

And finally, thank you to all my friends and family, who have given their patience and support throughout, especially: Sophie Lovell, Alicia Pivaro, Zoë Blackler, and Sandra Schaar; my husband, Chris; and my twin boys, Lucien and Wren, who have given up ever so much "mummy time" for this book.

Jenny Lovell

Introduction

A building's envelope, also known as its enclosure or facade, must reconcile many requirements—ventilation, solar heat gain, glare control, daylight levels, thermal insulation, water management, materials, assembly, sound and pollution control—making its design a complicated balancing act. However, the integration of environmental systems into a clear, comprehensive, and elegant design solution cannot be a Band-Aid application. It must be a synthesized and integral part of the design process, with a clear strategy that operates at multiple scales. Rather than acting as an instructional manual or a collection of case-study facts, Building Envelopes serves as a process-based tool kit of considerations for both practitioners and students to develop an integrated approach to the synthesis of design and technology in building envelopes.

This book directly stems from the "Hothouse" workshop that I taught at Washington University in St. Louis, and from a "Building Synthesis" course that I wrote, coordinated, and taught at the University of Virginia School of Architecture. It also has roots in my work as an architect, and it is intended as a bridge linking practice and academia. Through these two specific courses and my teaching in general, I have always endeavored to bring design and technology into one integrated forum.

Charged with preparing students for the profession, the design studios and technical courses of architecture degree programs offer the opportunity to change practice and perceptions within the market environment. Ideally, academia is the source of innovation in building design and implementation, since it primarily operates outside of the time and economic constraints of practice, but the current rapid pace of construction has positioned practice and industry to dominate the design and implementation of building envelopes. Form and performance of building envelopes are frequently compartmentalized in curricula and in professional practice.

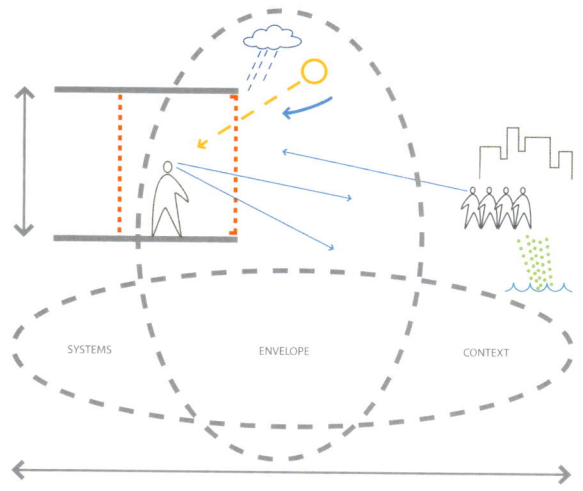

1| An architect's perspective: A building's envelope addresses the threshold between inside and out, between performance and form. There are a multitude of issues and influences that will come into play in designing an envelope that is both practical and elegant—from the building's program and users to its climate and context (community/surrounding buildings/environment/code) over its whole life cycle.

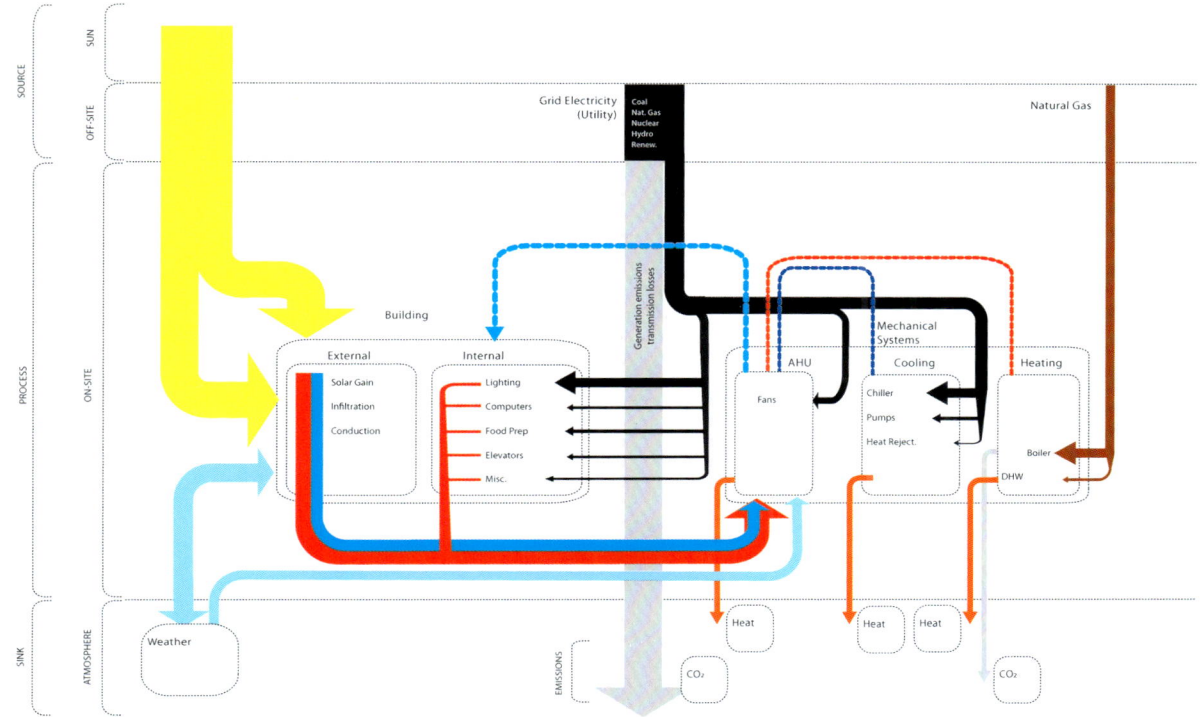

2 | An engineer's perspective: This diagram, by Matthew Herman of Buro Happold Consulting Engineers, shows the flow of source energy as it is processed through a building. The inefficiency of this process is output as waste that pollutes water and air. The goals of a building envelope's design should be to maximize the use of energy as it passes through the building and to minimize pollution. By understanding the relationships between the various systems that process energy and direct the flow through the system, it is possible to reduce or get rid of waste and inefficiencies.

However, if "best practice" examples and cutting-edge advances were discussed and explored within the academic realm as a form of research development, there would be a real opportunity for a sustainable, integrated mind-set to penetrate through education into practice (and vice versa).

Building Envelopes is organized into three sections. The first section, Feedback Loops of Form and Performance, establishes the criteria for an overall building envelope design strategy within the contexts of place, scale, performance, and time. The parts of the second section (Elements of a Holistic Approach)—air, heat, water, materials, daylighting, and energy—frame crises facing current practices and show solutions that can be implemented through good design, invention, and integration. The case studies in the third section, Integrated Building Envelope Strategies, offer examples of

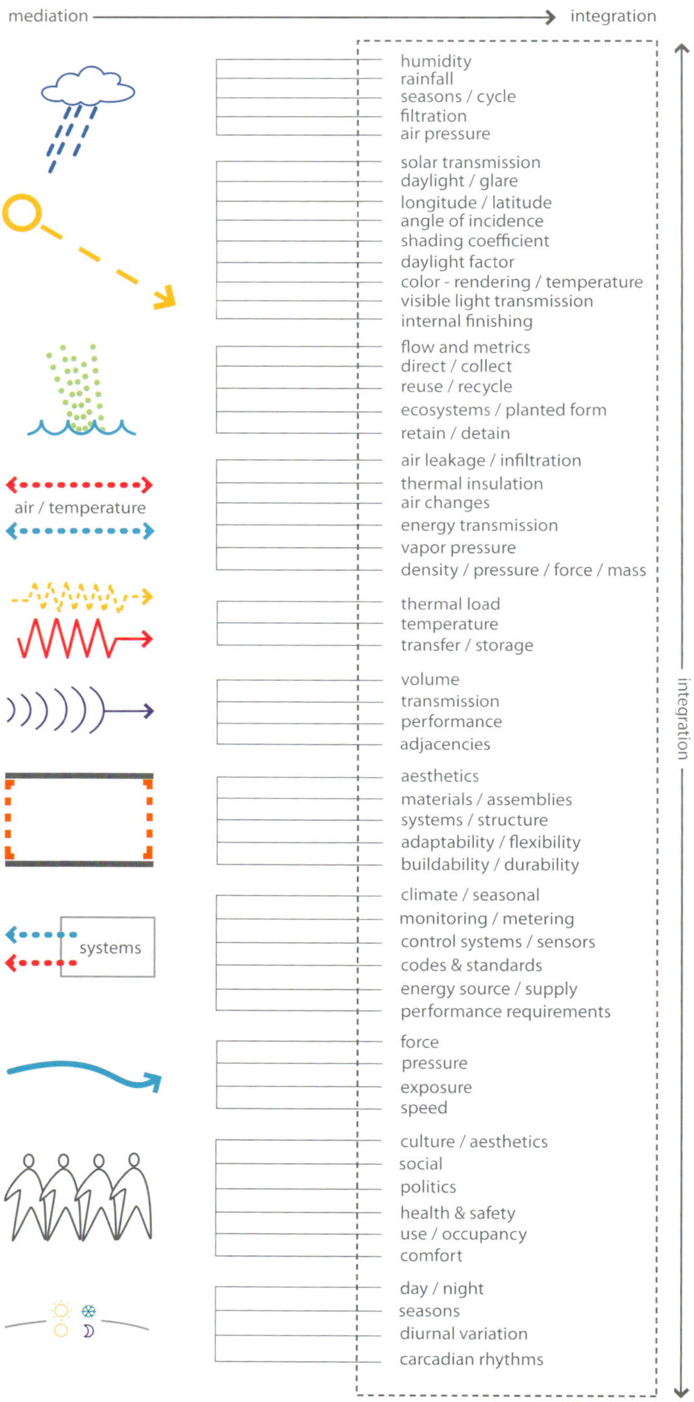

mediation ⟶ integration

- humidity
- rainfall
- seasons / cycle
- filtration
- air pressure

- solar transmission
- daylight / glare
- longitude / latitude
- angle of incidence
- shading coefficient
- daylight factor
- color - rendering / temperature
- visible light transmission
- internal finishing

- flow and metrics
- direct / collect
- reuse / recycle
- ecosystems / planted form
- retain / detain

- air leakage / infiltration
- thermal insulation
- air changes
- energy transmission
- vapor pressure
- density / pressure / force / mass

air / temperature

- thermal load
- temperature
- transfer / storage

- volume
- transmission
- performance
- adjacencies

- aesthetics
- materials / assemblies
- systems / structure
- adaptability / flexibility
- buildability / durability

- climate / seasonal
- monitoring / metering
- control systems / sensors
- codes & standards
- energy source / supply
- performance requirements

systems

- force
- pressure
- exposure
- speed

- culture / aesthetics
- social
- politics
- health & safety
- use / occupancy
- comfort

- day / night
- seasons
- diurnal variation
- carcadian rhythms

integration

Building Envelopes

14

built work that have achieved a poetic sensibility integrated with pragmatic application.

As we are increasingly made aware of our need to address and avert the environmental devastation of our planet, the elements described in the second section of this book are particularly relevant. Half of all the energy consumption and carbon dioxide emissions in the United States are attributed to buildings.[1] If we want to curb the negative impact of buildings on the environment, then building envelope design—from the nuts-and-bolts details of wall assemblies to the broader contexts of place and program—must be an essential part of this approach.

To enable a paradigm shift in the way we consider building envelopes, we must first realize the problems associated with the current state of affairs. The prevailing demand for sealed buildings with central air supplies prohibits users from controlling their internal environment. The market's desire for visual transparency through all-glass facades is in direct conflict with architects' responsibility to address the current environmental crisis. A building's envelope must integrate numerous systems and needs, yet most of all, it must relate to the scale and comfort of the human body and the dynamic nature of climate. As architects, we have to address and analyze complex sets of issues and relationships and reassemble them within the structure of a clear design strategy. Technology and design innovations should be utilized not for the creation of complex, preconceived forms or steady-state internal environments, but for adaptive and responsive thresholds of appropriate, responsible architecture.

opposite: Diagram Key
3 | This key shows how each of the icons depicted in the diagrams throughout the book should be read, as a collapsed composite of associated and multiple variables, by no means limited to the list shown here.

Section I: Feedback Loops of Form and Performance

How can the overall design, form, performance, and structure of a building envelope come together within a specific conceptual context? Recognizing that the best solutions are often the result of a holistic approach to the many and varied aspects of building design, this section focuses on the broad considerations of integrated form and performance. Matthias Sauerbruch—a partner in the renowned Anglo-German practice Sauerbruch Hutton who has written often of the delight of integrating design with the pragmatics of performance—recently stated that "Sustainability and bad design are contradictions in terms. It is the quality of architecture itself that contributes to both personal well-being and longevity of the built environment."[1] On this basis, this section begins by discussing the comfort and delight of the human body and goes on to give a clear understanding of the specific climates and contexts that a building envelope needs to address, including internal building requirements and the surrounding environment.

So much of a building's quality of life, delight, and performance depend on the initial stages of the design process, and these elements must therefore be considered as an overview to building envelope design. A building's design team, choice of building materials, fabrication, performance analysis, and life-cycle analysis all play a part in the creation of an integrated, sustainable building envelope.

Comfort at the Scale of the Body

> Mankind can exist, unassisted, on practically all those parts of the earth that are at present inhabited, except for the most arid and the most cold....But only just; in order to flourish, rather than merely survive, mankind needs more ease and leisure than a barefisted, and barebacked, single-handed struggle to exist could permit.
>
> –Reyner Banham, *The Architecture of the Well-tempered Environment*

Origins

The comfort range of the human body is somewhat limited, and it is dependant on activity and environmental circumstances. We originally evolved within a relatively narrow climate zone between the Tropic of Capricorn and the Tropic of Cancer, and then migrated to temperate climates, so comfort ranges are a product of our evolutionary history.[1] |1

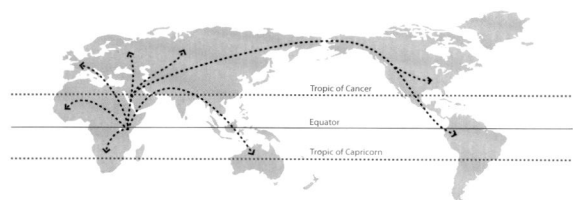

1| It is widely accepted that mankind originally evolved near the equator in Africa and migrated, as indicated on this world map, to temperate climates.

The human body moderates internal and external energy exchange through a complex set of balances in order to maintain the average 98.6 degrees Fahrenheit body temperature required for proper organ function. In buildings, heat radiating from computers, lights, people, and the sun (through the envelope), together with air temperature, humidity, and speed, combine to determine internal environmental conditions, which affect the body temperatures of occupants. We balance our metabolic rate by absorbing or emitting this heat in a constant state of energy exchange as the body attempts to achieve equilibrium. |2

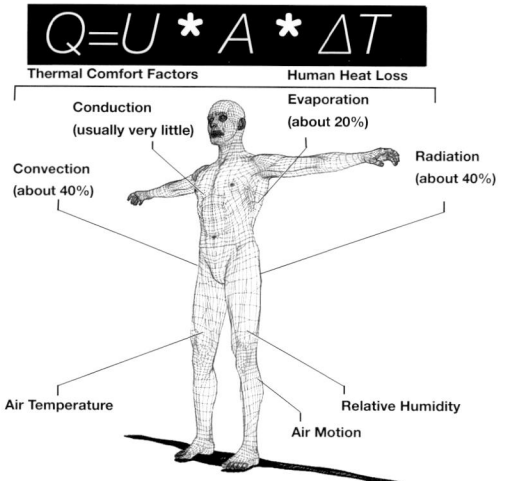

2| The equation of human thermal comfort factors, where "Q" equals energy, "U" equals conductance (rate of heat flow through an object), "A" equals area, and "ΔT" equals the change in temperature between a wall assembly separating interior and exterior environments: Conduction, convection, radiation, evaporation, air temperature, air motion, and relative humidity all influence this equation.

Why should the comfort of the human body be a starting point when considering the design of integrated building envelope strategies?

When a varied group of people live or work together in a building, its internal space—as defined by its envelope—has to account for both the individual and the collective through a multitude of parameters in order to achieve and maintain comfort. Comfort can be considered as a happiness of the mind and body, based on a wide range of

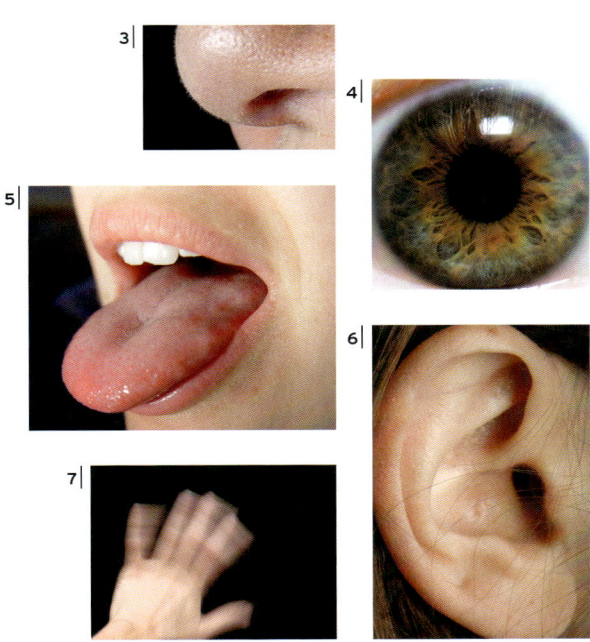

conditions that we experience through our senses—sight, hearing, taste, smell, and touch—as explained by engineer Max Fordham: "Our sensory responses let us know if we are comfortable, and thus effect our happiness."[2] |3-7

Comfort

The environmental conditions directly influenced by building envelope design that relate to comfort are temperature, humidity, light, sound, view, air flow, and air quality. Through building system standards, it is generally accepted that an internal temperature range of 68-78 degrees Fahrenheit, at 30-70 percent humidity, is a reasonable comfort zone for people against which building environmental systems can be measured.[3] |8 However, comfort is both more complex and more subtle than quantitative measures of temperature and relative humidity, and we are not limited to these ranges. Thermal comfort alone is defined by dynamic spatial conditions of internal and external temperature, humidity levels, and air velocity, together with factors related directly to an individual: clothing type, activity level, age, gender, health condition, metabolic rate, perception, and memory. |9-13 Over a period of a few weeks or months (such as seasonal changes), the human body can adjust its metabolism to live comfortably in a much wider range of temperatures than what we think of as "normal." This is called adaptive comfort.

Design developments in building envelopes and in heating, ventilation, and air conditioning (HVAC) systems over the past century have considerably shaped our tolerance for temperature fluctuations. Building envelopes can incorporate larger amounts of glazing, at the expense of mechanical systems required to offset heat gains or losses in order to maintain constant internal temperatures. The systems we tend to use to regulate our internal environments are based on control of an entire

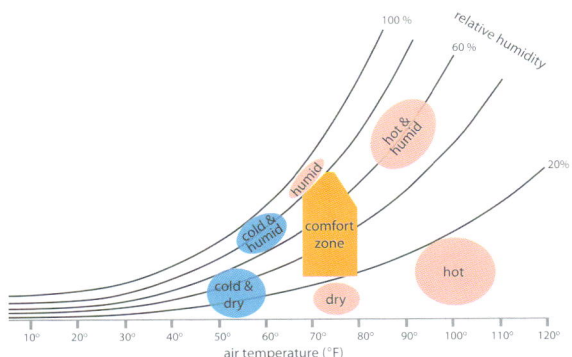

8| A psychrometric chart shows air temperature and humidity in relation to human comfort: The horizontal axis indicates air temperature, while the curved lines indicate relative humidity (RH)—the steeper the curve, the higher the RH. The zone of comfort shifts depending on temperature, air velocity, and human activity.

Feedback Loops of Form and Performance   19

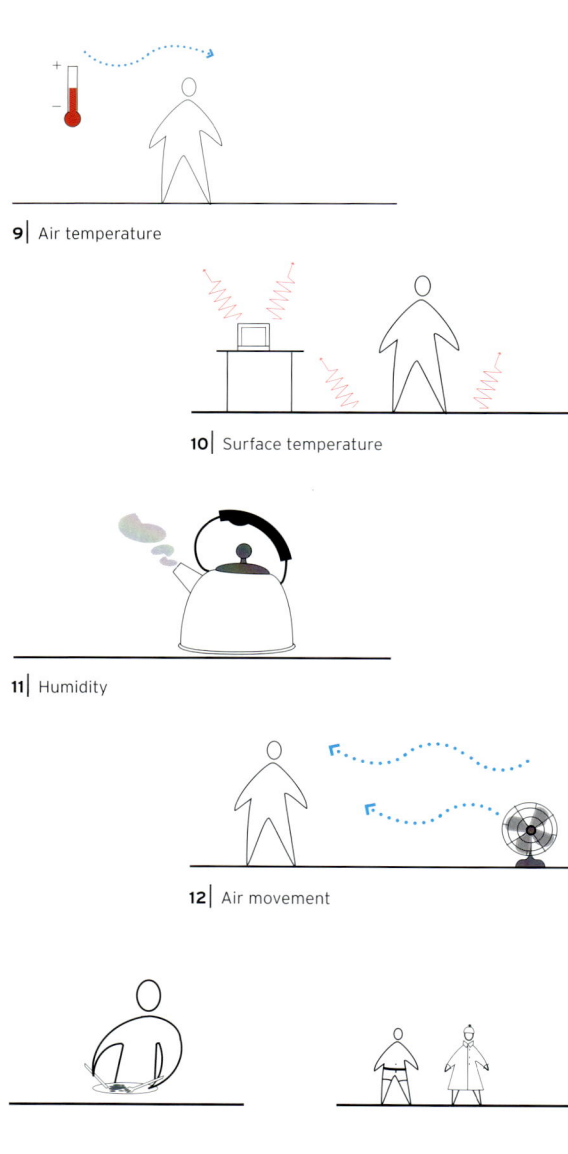

9 | Air temperature

10 | Surface temperature

11 | Humidity

12 | Air movement

13 | Metabolism, clothing, and activity: thermal comfort factors

space rather than individual-user control. For this reason, national building standards—as defined by the American Society of Heating, Refrigerating and Air-Conditioning Engineers (ASHRAE) regulation 55-2004—require that 80 percent of all building occupants exposed to the same conditions within a space must be "comfortable" at any given time.[4]

Adaptability

By nature, we do not expect our environment to maintain a constant, air-conditioned, seventy-two-degree-Fahrenheit temperature. Our perception of comfort is quite adaptive and is based on circumstance, expectation of environmental conditions, and activity. These dictate our clothing choices—if it's hot we wear less clothing, and if it's cold we bundle up! Our ability to adjust to different temperature ranges within normal seasonal changes is dictated by what feels comfortable, and, across different geographical regions, what constitutes a warm or cold day. For example, sixty-five degrees Fahrenheit feels very different in January versus in July, or for a person from Phoenix versus a person from Juneau. We are not only limited to the standard comfort range of sixty-eight to seventy-eight degrees Fahrenheit, which relates to industrial-age humans with central heating and cooling systems. This range would not have applied to most of the world's population, say, a couple of centuries ago.[5] Our bodies have their own mechanisms with which to modulate heat, such as evaporative cooling through sweating and breathing. |14 If we know and expect our internal environment to fluctuate, we can individually adapt our bodies (within reason) to maintain comfort levels within a much wider temperature and humidity range than what is generally expected to be achieved in air-conditioned buildings.

Building Envelopes   20

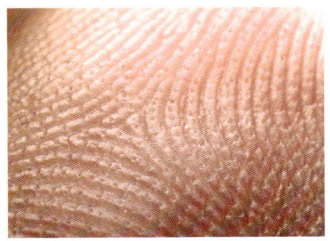

14 Skin, the surface of exchange

Comfort, Space and Control

Office spaces, where people can spend more than forty hours a week, must address comfort and allow for flexibility of control from day to day, season to season, and year to year. If you can achieve comfort for 80 percent of occupants in an office building through systems integration, this may be attributed in large part to its envelope, but a better design could help narrow the satisfaction gap for the remaining 20 percent of occupants. Enabling users to control their environment in some way—for example, by allowing them to open and close a window or to activate shading devices for heat gain and glare control—can further improve individual comfort.

Unit residential designs lack the higher numbers of people, computers, and lighting levels found in work environments, so heat gained through internal loads is not as much of a concern. Spaces are usually smaller than in offices, and building envelope strategies can be developed to address specific and more varied program requirements such as eating, sleeping, washing, cooking, and relaxing.

Of course, comfort in both office and residential design involves more than just thermal conditions—it encompasses indoor air quality, light levels, acoustics, ergonomics, and materials for furniture, fixtures, and fittings, as well as the ability to control and access views. Each of these factors has a specific set of requirements, which vary according to a given program or location. It may be pleasant, for example, to have some west light coming in through a living room window at the end of the day, but for an office this is likely to lead to discomfort from glare and heat gain.

A building envelope is an active threshold, "A zone in which change occurs."[6] It is responsible for, among other things, modulating between outside and inside conditions to achieve comfort for the human beings within. Since about 35 percent of a building's construction budget might be spent on its envelope, it is a good place to passively and actively control energy transfer to create occupant comfort and reduce energy consumption. Thus, it is essential to consider comfort in relation to the human body as well as the potential of a building envelope's design within the context of its environmental variables in order to achieve an optimum overall integrated design strategy.

Climate and Context

Only when understanding our place, we may be able to participate creatively and contribute to its history.
–Christian Norberg-Schulz, *Genius Loci: Towards a Phenomenology of Architecture*

Site Specific

Every building envelope project is like a bespoke suit, to be tailored to its specific set of circumstances. |1 No matter what advances are made in digital design, prefabrication, and modular construction, the envelope of any building still ultimately has a unique set of external and internal environmental criteria that it must engage, mediate, and adapt.

A building's envelope serves two primary conditions: it has to enclose and make sense of the internal volume it contains, and it has to delineate and characterize external space. There is invariably a distinction between the obligations of these inner and outer conditions, and the surface depth of a building must respond to both conditions.[1] In terms of external space, the building envelope has to relate to micro- and macro-environments: orientation, exposure, ground conditions, adjacencies, and climate, as well as to the existing historical, cultural, and social contexts of a specific place.

To successfully design a building's massing, envelope, and material, structural, and system

1| Like a suit, a building's envelope must be tailored to its specific context of location—from climate to use and inhabitation—in order to get the most adaptive fit.

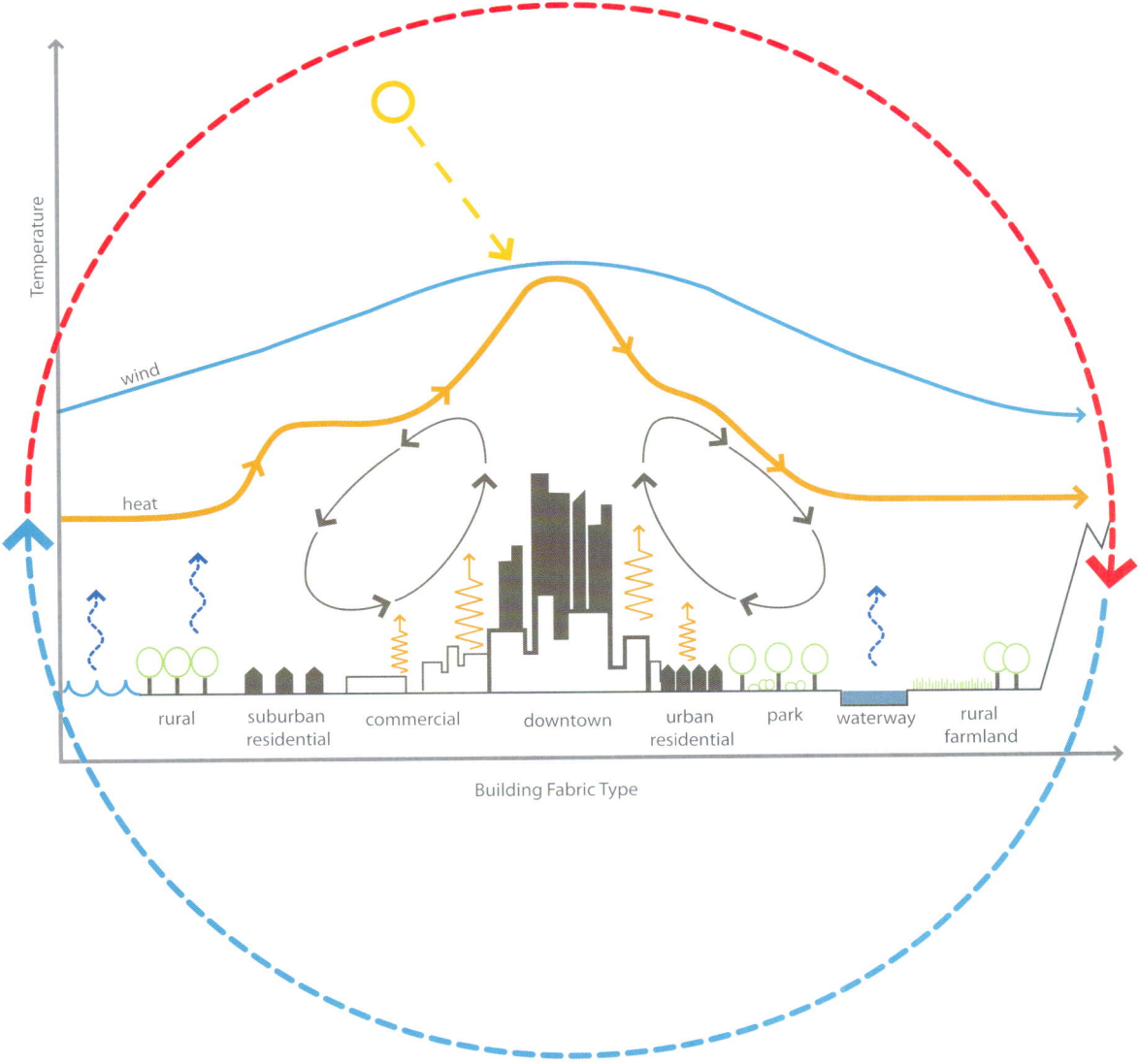

2 | Building envelopes must act as a filter between internal and external environments, enabling internal environmental control through engagement, mediation, and adaptation. The external environment is not only governed by climate alone, but also by a number of issues related to adjacencies, such as urban development and bodies of water. As this diagram shows, an urban microclimate generally has higher temperatures than a rural one, due to a "heat island" effect created by the additional built surfaces and waste energy of densely inhabited areas. The gray arrow loops indicate unstable circulating currents at the edge of urban microclimates, where cool and warm air meet. The whole temperature cycle, indicated by the blue and magenta outer loop, is not constant, but is in a state of flux between day and night and by season. For example, temperature differences between urban and rural areas are generally greatest during evenings and in winter.

applications, we must know and understand the environment and context for which we are designing. The environment that a building serves is fundamentally governed by temperature, air pressure, and humidity. Changes to these elements are the result of energy transfer through convection, radiation, or conduction, and, depending on the specific circumstances of the location, must be understood as dynamic conditions with which a building envelope needs to engage. Different locations in the world, with their specific climatic conditions, inevitably present different priorities between temperature and humidity through the seasons—as do individual site locations and adjacencies. |2

Data Collection and Flow
On April 1, 1960, the polar-orbiting satellite TIROS 1 (the first in the series of Television and Infrared Observation Satellites) was launched, marking the beginning of the collection of satellite weather data, which supplement records organized by networks of terrestrial weather stations. Meteorological data has been systematically recorded for over a century, and developments in communication and recording systems have hugely expanded the collection of these information sets. These data collections describe patterns of general weather conditions, such as temperatures and precipitation levels, together with more extreme events, such as hurricanes, droughts, and tornados. Climatic weather zones also relate weather to specific soil and vegetation patterns across the world. |3

Data recorded over the last fifty years or so has been compiled in a computer-compatible format and creates the basis for ongoing records, from which architects and engineers can establish performance criteria and against which they can measure building-simulation analyses. This information, which can truly alter our understanding of how a building might perform in a given place, is now

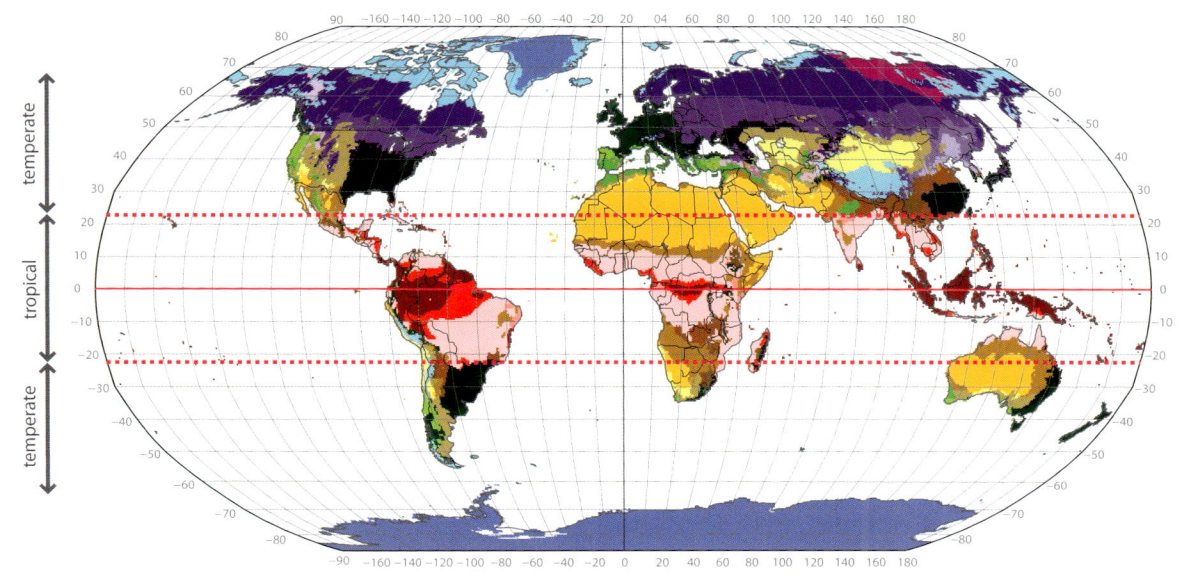

Main climates

A: equatorial
B: arid
C: temperate
D: continental
E: polar

Precipitation

W: desert
S: steppe
f: fully humid

s: summer dry
w: winter dry
m: monsoonal

Temperature

h: hot arid
k: cold arid
a: hot summer
b: warm summer

c: cool summer
d: extremely continental
F: polar frost
T: polar tundra

updated with CRU TS 2.1 temperature and VASClimO v1.1 precipitation data 1951 to 2000

3 | The Köppen climate classification scheme (c. 1900) divides world climates into five main groups (equatorial/arid/temperate/continental/polar) and several types and subtypes related to vegetation, precipitation, and temperature.

Feedback Loops of Form and Performance   25

readily available through a vast array of sources, including internet-enabled weather stations that stream live data directly to building management systems, energy models, energy management systems, facade actuators, and any other system that uses environmental conditions as part of its logic control or decision-making process to determine its optimized position or configuration.[2]

It is important for data relating to climate and context to be assessed by multiple sources, and not to be accepted at face value. Data-collection methods and criteria may vary, and comparison enables a check on anomalies that may not be apparent from reviewing a single source. Databases such as EnergyPlus compile weather data from as many as twenty sources. However, this information is likely to be based on a single location—say, an airport or downtown—and may not take into account localized conditions such as heat islands, lake cooling, or wind tunnels created by immediate surroundings.

Application and Resources
Why is climate-data collection and processing important? What does it mean for a building envelope to address one set of external conditions over another? As demand for fossil fuels increases and availability decreases, and as the effects of global warming become more apparent, energy consumption becomes more critical. Building envelopes must (more than) mediate between external climatic conditions and people's comfort. By optimizing a building's envelope, we can manipulate the heat gain or loss of a building and reduce energy consumption. |4

In the last century, the development of mechanical systems for the internal environmental control of buildings has required more energy than ever needed before by humans, provided by the burning of fossil fuels. Through this increased dependence on mechanical systems to control our internal environment, building envelopes have

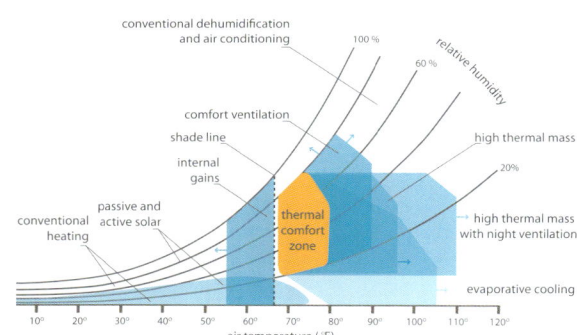

4| This diagram takes the psychrometric chart from page 19 and elaborates on it to show the effectiveness of different design strategies in "pushing the envelope" of the conventional comfort zone (pictured in orange). The blue areas show the extent to which various strategies can extend the potential comfort zone. For example, high thermal mass of the building combined with a nighttime ventilation strategy can considerably enlarge the comfort zone, depending on the specifics of context.

been somewhat freed from the responsibilities of addressing climate, causing an irresponsible "flattening" of environmental expectations by building users. People expect constancy in a building's temperature and humidity, rather than being willing to cope with fluctuations. The specifics of place have been subverted by a global adoption of the glass box envelope, but the performance requirements of that glass box in, say, Dubai versus in New York are utterly different in their need to balance daylight, glare, and potential heat gain or loss. Aside from differences in latitude and longitude and local climate, diurnal variations—maximum and minimum values of temperature, pressure, relative humidity, and so on during a solar day—have a considerable effect on a building's envelope and systems performances. How hard will the envelope and internal systems have to work to achieve comfort levels? How much energy will they require?

Analysis Goals
We can now use sophisticated weather-data collection to assess the suitability of design strategies. Advances in computer technologies enable analyses that used to be laborious and costly at best, and impossible at worst. Computer software packages such as eQUEST or Ecotect have increasingly user-friendly design interfaces that enable building envelope strategies to be tested in terms of performance in a specific location over time (see Building Simulation Tools, pp. 42–48, for more information on these programs). |5 By using this knowledge and testing prior to, during, and after design, we can establish site-appropriate responses that work with our environment and not against it.

What does all this environmental data show us? The presentation of a wind rose or psychometric chart as a preface to envelope and massing design proposals is meaningless unless placed in the context of its implication. For example, wind roses show

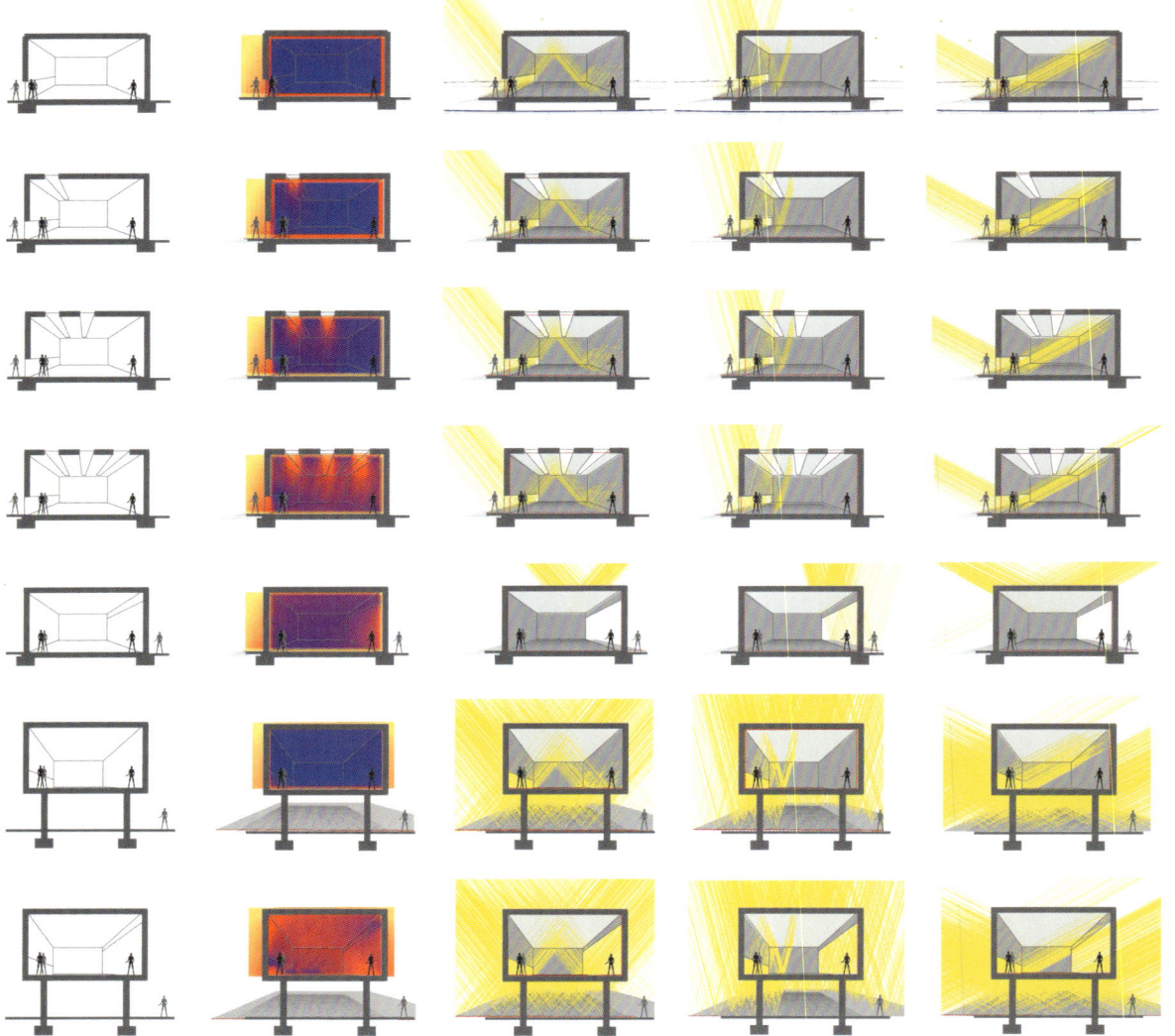

5 | Spatial organization and lighting options are tested for an office building, produced using Autodesk Ecotect software. Primary explorations show window openings at different orientations and at varying section levels from the walls to the roof. From left to right, the studies above show: the building section with different window options, annual light levels, spring/fall light levels, summer light levels, and winter light levels.

opposite:
6 | Wind rose charts map cumulative annual as well as seasonal prevailing winds in order to maximize ventilation strategies for a project in St. Louis.

Building Envelopes

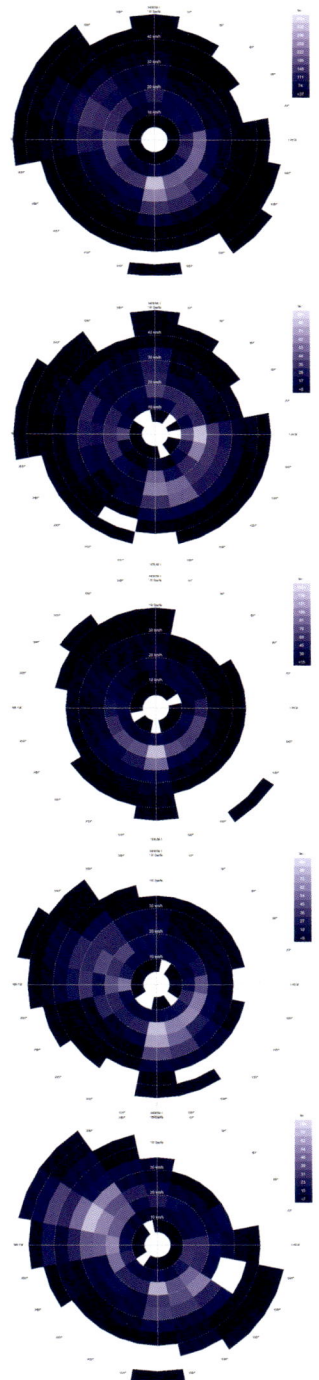

us the wind frequency and speed from a specific direction through the year, based on thirty years of weather-data collection. |6 In terms of building envelope design, this indicates the prevailing winds for each season, and therefore we can start to work out where and when breezes might be harnessed for ventilation or reducing heat gain.

Climate conditions must be analyzed and, through a design strategy, synthesized into a means of internal comfort over time. With ever-expanding amounts of data and sources of information available, it becomes more and more critical to frame an "analysis goal"—a focus for data review and building simulation, to establish the priorities for a design process.

Climate and weather are fluid conditions: the dynamic nature of the environment must be incorporated into a design response in the form of daily, seasonal, and annual cycles of heat transfer, air pressure changes, and humidity levels. |7 Above all, systems, construction, assembly, and materials should be considered as part of a context of place, idea, and solution at the earliest stages of the design process.

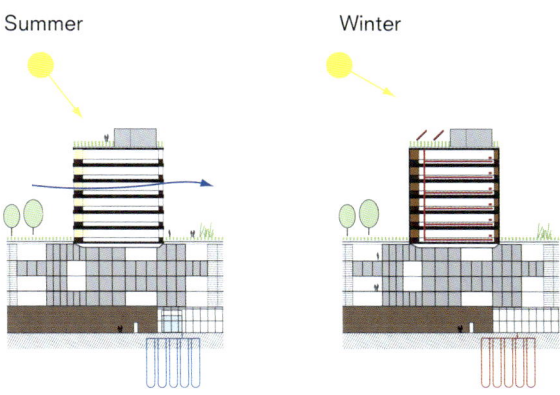

7| Diagrams produced by SHoP Architects indicate summer and winter design strategies for heating and cooling.

Feedback Loops of Form and Performance

Interdisciplinary to Transdisciplinary

> Architecture requires us constantly to reinterpret and revalue technology in human and social terms...close-knit, interdisciplinary design teams are necessary to confront the scale and complexity of modern buildings if an architecture is to survive which embodies humane ideas.
>
> –Sir Philip Dowson, *Arup Associates: The Biography of an Architectural Practice*

With greater complexity in architecture comes a greater level of specialization. A typical design team might be composed of architects, structural engineers, environmental engineers, lighting consultants, envelope performance specialists, acoustic consultants, and many others—the list is expanding. Considering the breadth and depth of expertise required as systems and possibilities grow at an exponential rate, an architect, now more than ever, needs to be aware of processes and technologies that will impact the perception, experience, and performance of a building, and be able to then synthesize these voices into a clear design strategy.

Collaboration

While teaching an integrated technology course at the University of Virginia, I arranged for a number of consultants to come into the classroom and design studio over the semester. Visitors included some of the industry's most respected structural and environmental engineers and cladding manufacturers. About midway through the course, one frustrated architecture student asked, "Why do we have to meet all these people? I just want to design my building envelope!" In architecture schools, design is generally a solo operation; students are not used to working with engineers or other consultants in a team scenario. However, in practice, architects invariably work in collaboration with other specialists. The point of having all these consultants visit the classroom/studio was to show that architects cannot, and do not, operate in a vacuum—a fact that the graduates quickly realized after they began practicing full time.

The design and systems integration required in a building envelope (especially in a larger building envelope) is increasingly more complex, and it cannot be achieved successfully without collaborators. In order to achieve comfortable environments and have a more sustainable approach to envelope design within a specific context, it is important that a building's architects and engineers work together from the earliest stages of the design process. This defines integrated design, which is as much about the assembly of a team and an architect's ability to have peripheral vision over a project as it is about realizing a conceptual design.

In the United Kingdom, clients usually directly hire key design team members—i.e., architects and engineers—whereas in the United States, 95 percent of engineers for buildings are appointed through the architect (according to a 2005 AIA Survey). Aesthetic, environmental, and structural strategies are inseparable in an integrated building envelope design—if the design process is driven by a client or an architect with a desire to create an "icon" building derived from complex form-making, then the mechanical services and engineering will be required to reconcile that form with the environment. This process runs the risk of leading to Band-Aid solutions, where engineers hired later in the design process end up fixing problems rather than working across disciplines at an earlier stage to avoid those issues, or to realize them as opportunities.

Facade Engineering
With increased complexity in and contractual responsibility for larger, more complex building envelope designs, design specialists (as teams within larger firms or stand-alone consultants) can also be part of a design team. For example, a facade

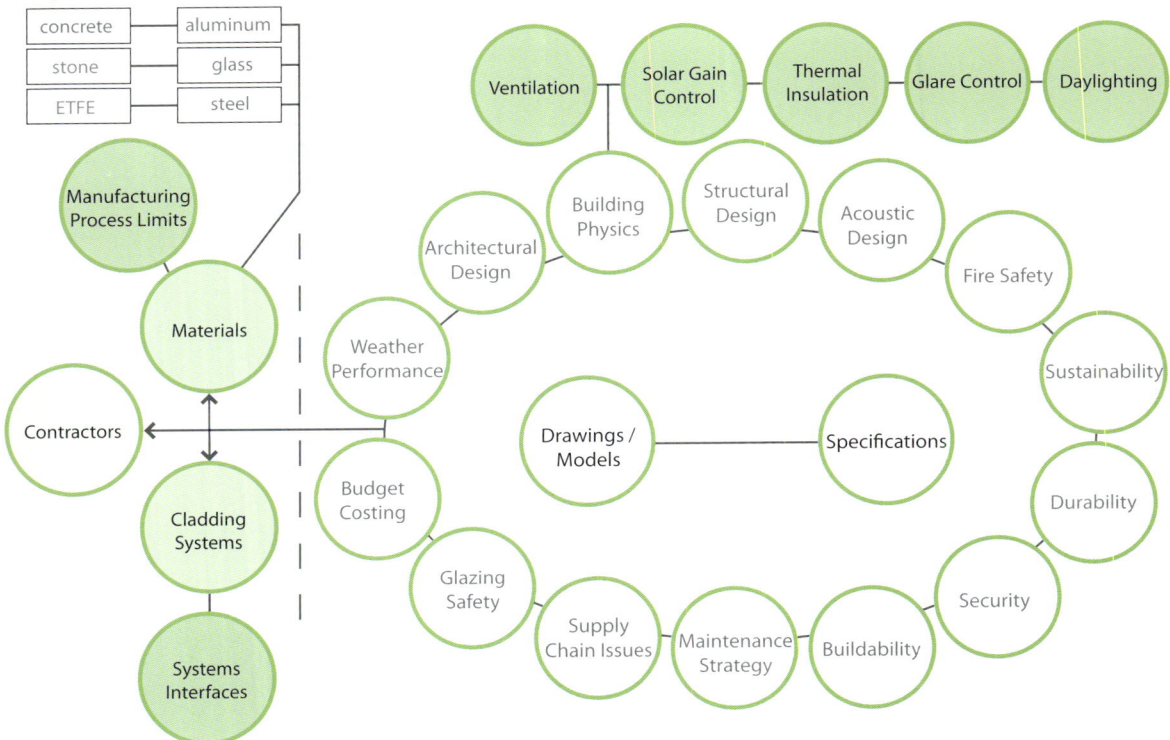

1| Buro Happold's facade-engineering team diagrammed how the elements of a multidisciplinary, integrated building envelope strategy are interrelated.

consultant (often working within an engineering practice) offers expertise in the analysis and detail development of an envelope, including the use of computational fluid dynamics to understand air flows and pressure differentials, as well as finite element analysis of a structure.

Facade engineers at multidisciplinary firm Buro Happold have mapped out the components that have to be fully integrated for the design of a building envelope. |1 The bubble diagram shown represents a methodology to analyze a building envelope's design in a comprehensive and systematic way. Each of the subject headings in the bubbles represents a whole field of study, which opens up new bubbles specific to it, as shown in the case of "Building Physics." New bubbles are added as new technology and design priorities demand. This diagram is an attempt to document everything that influences and contributes to the successful engineering of a facade. Two bubbles—"Drawings/Models" and "Specifications"—are enclosed within the ring of subjects to acknowledge that all these influences are ultimately captured in a set of documents. These are passed to the contractor—shown on the left-hand side of the diagram—and the design is then expressed in terms of the materials and systems available or required and, again, represents a host of considerations. Importantly, the interfaces between all systems should be carefully considered and coordinated before the contractor fabricates, tests, and installs the facade.

Associations

Another way of considering the format of interdisciplinary relationships is as a matrix relating to the scale at which disciplines work; one that is not based on a linear process but relates to associated subject fields, where the density of concentration would shift depending on the specific circumstances of a project. Thinking laterally across fields and understanding each specialist's scale of operation can greatly enhance the possibility of association. For example, a material scientist might be working at the molecular scale and an environmentalist at the scale of a whole ecosystem—depending on the specifics of the project, the relationships of these scales of investigation can allow new possibilities for an integrated design. |2 To enable real invention, we need to make a paradigm shift from the business-as-usual multidisciplinary and interdisciplinary team structure to transdisciplinary ways of working on a team.[1] Transdisciplinary work is a far more fluid process with shared responsibility.

Deep Collaboration

The building industry pretty much works in a multidisciplinary way now—participants and their input

	eco/geological	infrastructure	building-macro	interior/spatial	ergonomic	structural	mechanical	microscopic	molecular	nanoscopic	
conceptual programming	+	+	+	+	+	+	+	+			ARCHITECTURE
schematic design	+	+	+	+	+	+	+	+	+	+	
cross disciplinary coordination	+	+	+	+	+	+	+	+	+	+	
integrated building systems	+	+	+	+	+	+	+	+			
design development	+	+	+	+	+	+	+	+	+	+	
net building energy flows	+	+	+	+	+	+	+	+	+		
environmental control systems	+	+	+	+	+	+	+	+	+	+	MECHANICAL ENGINEERING
optical engineering	+	+	+	+	+	+	+	+	+		
mechatronics	+	+	+	+	+	+	+	+			
heat transfer	+	+	+	+	+	+	+	+	+	+	
manufacturing	+	+	+	+	+	+	+				
environmental control systems	+	+	+	+	+	+	+	+			ELECTRICAL ENGINEERING
semiconductors	+	+	+	+		+	+	+	+		
nanotechnology	+	+	+	+			+	+	+	+	
energy optimization	+	+	+	+	+	+	+				
microelectronics	+	+	+	+	+	+	+	+			

2| Created by the Center for Architecture Science and Ecology (CASE), this transdisciplinary diagram shows which disciplines participate in different scales of building research development. The y axis shows activity range specific to discipline (outlined on right, in detail on left), while the x axis shows which scale they are working at. This diagram was developed to represent the team-working relationships for the Integrated Concentrating (IC) system (see pp. 94-95).

Feedback Loops of Form and Performance

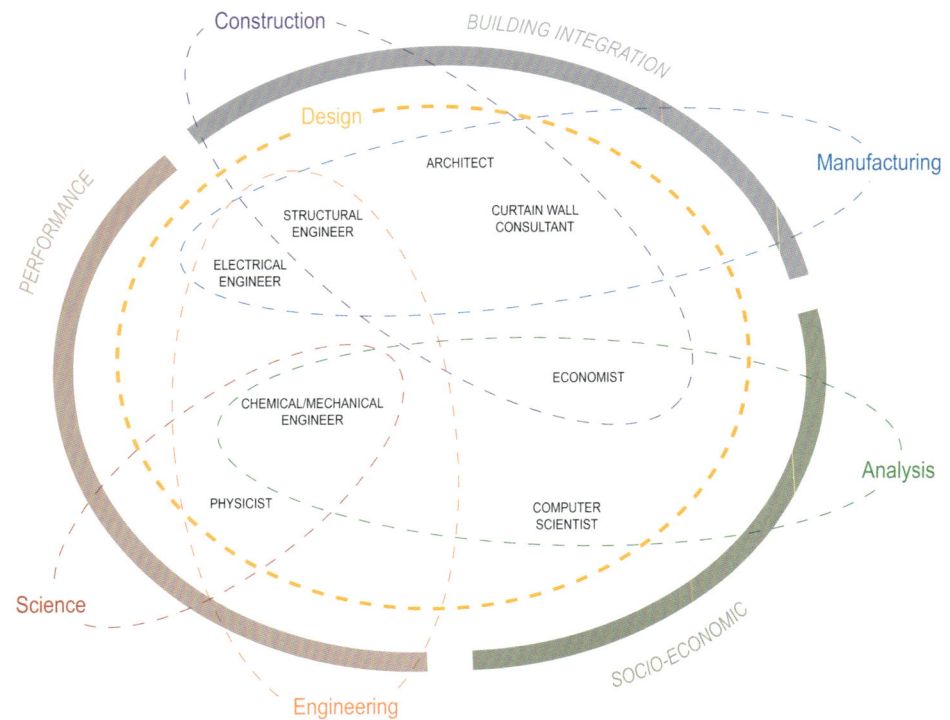

3 | Transdisciplinary team integration as mapped by CASE for the development of the IC system. This shows the fluid nature of transdicsiplinary teamwork, where the problem brings everyone together through the many crossovers in the design process.

are tracked in clear, distinct categories, primarily related to liability and responsibility—to allow for finger pointing if anything goes wrong. This structure of responsibility and control is inhibiting, and it keeps design teams from pushing boundaries. Integrated design through interdisciplinary practice is a collaboration developed across a team— for example, when a lighting engineer works with a facade engineer to maximize daylight use and control at the perimeter of a building. This kind of interdisciplinary team structure is considered "best practice."

Transdisciplinarity, however, is an approach that is hard to realize in the building industry as it currently operates, because it requires levels of trust from all parties, new kinds of teams, and new legal relationships. Transdisciplinarity "recognizes the role of values in inquiry, [and] rather than attempting to suppress or 'bracket' them, it engages

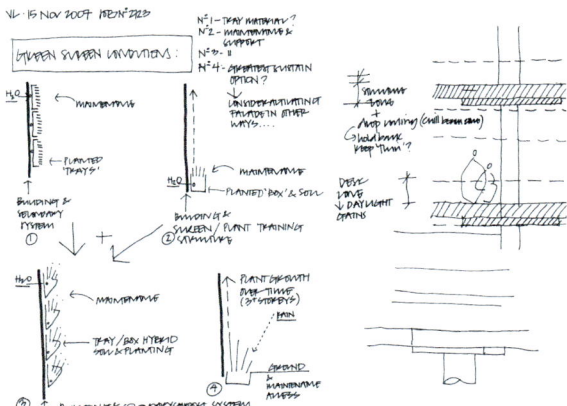

4 | Sketches drawn by the author while consulting with William McDonough + Partners, during a meeting with Rana Creek to review green screen options

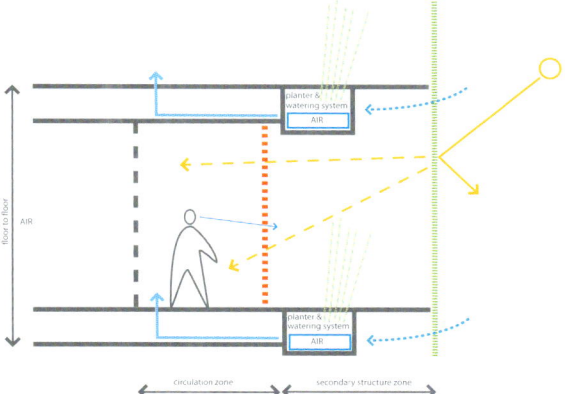

5 | Diagram of a green wall strategy, based on the author's sketches (Figure 4), that shows the possibility of integrating shading and air-cooling strategies in a building envelope by integrating a green screen (a planted shading strategy) with air intake on an exposed southwest facade. Incoming air could be drawn across the root zone of the plantings to cool and humidify air in a warm, dry climate.

the inquirer as an active ethical participant."[2] An extended team rallies around problems in search of the best solutions possible. This is deep collaboration—idea exchange in an unanticipated way, with a free flow of information—that may enable experimental work leading to new solutions but can also be unwieldy in terms of the time demands for development and testing of new ideas. For transdisciplinary work to be possible, we would have to "structurally rethink industry, institutions and practice," and put aside claims to intellectual property ownership—full collaboration would be necessary.[3] |3

Collaboration is increasingly being made across fields of expertise, and it relates to much broader fields of knowledge. When I consulted at William McDonough + Partners we often discussed possible building envelope design solutions with scientists, ecologists, planners, and even horticultural specialists—for example, a meeting with Rana Creek, a consultancy specializing in environmental planning and sustainable design, covered topics from "green screen" implementation strategies to a far-more-integrated possibility of running air intake through planting systems to absorb heat before it was drawn into the interior. |4-5

Collaboration between disciplines and industry is required from the earliest possible stage in the design process for integrated design, including, importantly, contractors and fabricators. Depending on the form of a building's contract, the people who will be constructing the project can be brought in at the beginning stages of design development. The fabricator and/or contractor can be given a "design assist" role, meaning that rather than waiting to bid on a project based on a full set of construction documents from the design team, the contractor and fabricators can come to the table early on in the process—bringing effective design influence to assembly, coordination, and buildability. In all of the case studies included in the third section of this book, the contractor (to a lesser or greater degree) was brought in to the design process earlier than a traditional program would dictate.

A building's envelope cannot afford to be a passive facade. It is not merely an object or wallpaper—it takes engineering input and integration between form and performance to create a solution that goes beyond simple mediation of inside and outside conditions. We need to ask the right questions to tackle the challenge of ever broadening and deepening technology applications and to decide what is appropriate for both the specific and general needs of a project. The ability to frame questions is fundamental to working collaboratively across fields toward a transdiciplinary objective and creating possibilities that are above and beyond "business as usual" for building envelopes.

Materials and Fabrication

By integrating design, analysis, manufacture and the assembly of building around digital technologies, architects, engineers and builders have an opportunity to fundamentally redefine the relationships between conception and production.

—Branko Kolarevic, *Architecture in the Digital Age: Design and Manufacturing*

For figures 1 to 4: These building envelopes (all designed by architect Peter Zumthor) achieve the pragmatic requirements of construction—they keep water out, transfer structural loads, hold in heat or cold, can be cleaned, and can be built—but they present very different architectural responses in terms of form and materiality, borne out of their varied contexts.

Architectural design has the potential for a multitude of construction and technological responses, the majority of which are driven by factors far beyond the proverbial drawing board. Design is a fundamental determinant of how a building looks, but if you want to achieve success on-site, appropriate realization of this design from the multitude of available and emerging materials, assemblies, and technologies must be considered. The exploration of building construction within an academic setting, however, often removes much of the pragmatics of practice.

1| Bregenz Art Museum, Bregenz, Austria, 1997

2| Vals Thermal Baths, Graubünden, Switzerland, 1996

3| Shelters for a Roman archaeological site, Chur, Graubünden, Switzerland, 1986

4| Gugalun Truog House, Versam, Graubünden, Switzerland, 1994

In my undergraduate construction course, the class focuses on basic building principles, techniques, materials, and the relationship between envelope and structure. Construction principles are reviewed from the perspective of aesthetic intent together with the necessity for pragmatic responses to the complex issues of site, context, and program. These two approaches are not set out as binary or opposing conditions, as they have tended to be in contemporary architecture curricula, but rather as part of a holistic solution to place and program that privileges their balance over the deterrence of one or the other. Students are encouraged to "unpack" their studio projects in terms of a sequence of assembly and to diagram how materials are connected rather than approaching design as purely aesthetic object-making. This exercise enables integrated resolution through design context and process, rather than the application of material choices and construction strategies as separate considerations. |1-4

Palette
The choice of materials and assembly systems for a building envelope is governed by a varied set of criteria, from context to building use, performance to identity. Reliance upon mechanical systems to control the internal environments of buildings combined with developments in digital modeling and fabrication (CAD/CAM) have enabled an approach of "material as visual artifact," where a palette can be freely applied solely on a visual basis, and the superficial creation of complex and seductive form is possible with little regard for environmental performance.[1] The specification of materials is often a "pick-n-mix" exercise rather than an integration of the most appropriate materials and fabrication techniques for both the form and performance of a building in a specific context.

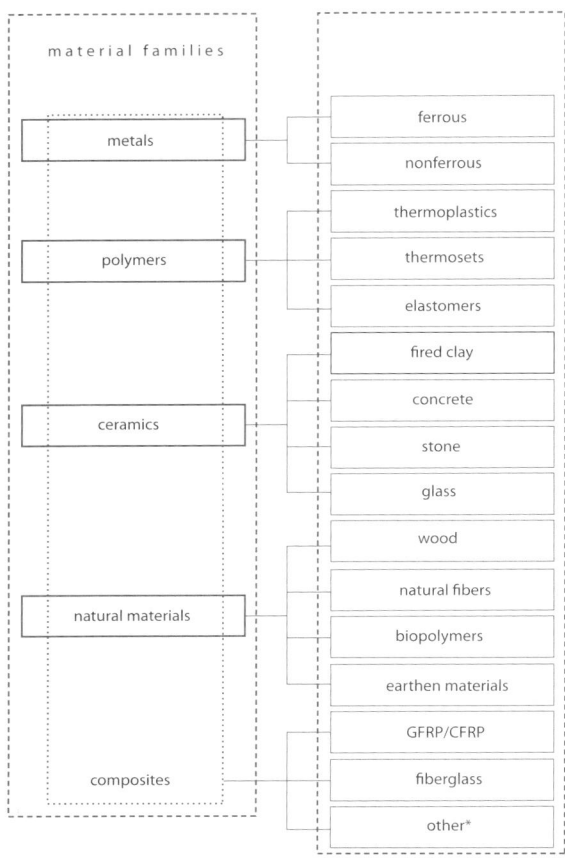

*Composites include metal/metal, ceramic/ceramic, ceramic/metal, polymer/metal, and many other types. GFRP, CFRP and fiberglass are all examples of fiber reinforced polymers (FRP).

5| Classification of material families and common materials used in building construction, developed by Associate Professor John Fernandez (MIT) from multiple sources

Energy transfer through a building envelope is determined by the architect's choice of materials and assembly design, as well as by internal and external environmental conditions. The designer is responsible for subtly choreographing the integral relationships between material properties, appropriate specifications, form, construction, and performance over the life span of a building. A materials palette is not about separate applications, but rather how materials can be integrated to meet the poetic and pragmatic intent of a building's envelope design.

Properties

Materials are categorized into families of specific properties: metals, polymers, ceramics, organics, and composites. Even within a given family, the range of material properties can be substantial. |**5** For example, while stainless steel and aluminum might be specified for their resistance to corrosion, stainless steel is almost four times denser and has five times the tensile strength of aluminum.[2] Material scientists, engineers, and architects have very different ways of categorizing these properties, but what they have in common in terms of building envelope design is a need for appropriate application.

The intrinsic properties of materials—their strength, toughness, thermal conductivity, porosity, and chemical reactivity—affect how they can be brought together within an assembly or system and how they will perform in a given environment.[3] Combined with these properties are the broader economic, environmental, social, and cultural implications of a material, such as: Where is it sourced from? How much will it cost? How will it be maintained? How is it perceived? How does it relate to the building's context? How does it perform relative to the climate? |**6-9**

Building Envelopes   38

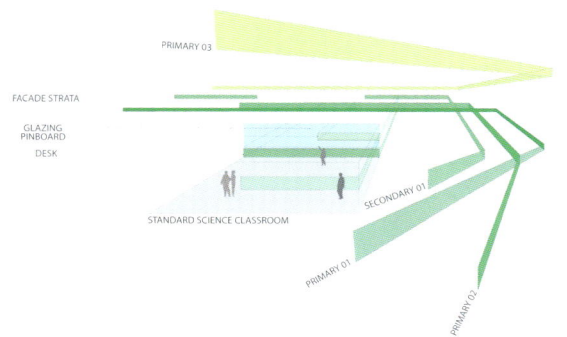

For figures 6-9: Allford Hall Monaghan Morris chose glazed terracotta tiles for the envelope of Westminster Academy—a secondary school in London—for their performance, buildability, appearance, and context. The architects wanted to create a landmark building and give a positive identity to this tough, inner-city neighborhood, which is surrounded by austere gray housing blocks and busy roads. The shades of green tile get lighter toward the sky, and each stratum of color also relates to the internal organization of the school. At ground level, the material is robust enough to cope with wear and tear as well as potential vandalism (it's difficult to mark or paint on), and panels of tile can easily be replaced if they are damaged.

6 | Envelope and color concept diagram

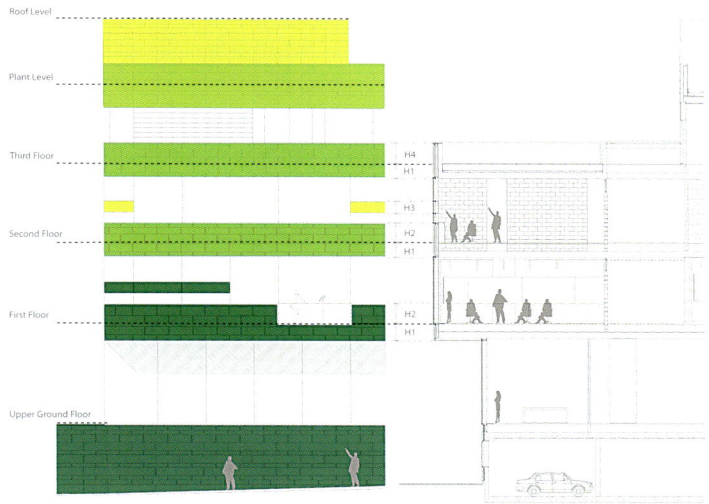

7 | Color palette of the glazed terracotta tiles

8 | Elevation detail

9 | North facade, glass balustrade detail

Feedback Loops of Form and Performance

10 | Cladding mock-up for the IAC Building, Permasteelisa/Gehry Partners, New York, New York

11 | Cladding mock-up for Hearst Tower, Permasteelisa/Foster + Partners, New York, New York

12 | Cladding mock-up for 7 World Trade Center, Permasteelisa/Skidmore, Owings & Merrill with James Carpenter Design Associates, New York, New York

13 | Cladding mock-up for the Institute of Criminology, Grupa Schneider/Allies and Morrison, Cambridge, England

Testing

Multiple performance characteristics of materials and assemblies can be tested using digital modeling to refine specifications, but ultimately a building must be built properly to meet these requirements. The only way to test how well a building will be constructed is through mock-ups and continual reviews on-site while the building is being made. Visual and performance mock-ups are full-scale constructions of part of a building envelope assembly that incorporate the actual specified materials. Whether made using a stick system (where components are assembled on-site) or unitized panels (using prefabricated, large-scale units), building envelopes must be weathertight, i.e., resist water penetration to the interior, control air leakage and condensation, and resist wind loads. Each of these criteria has testing procedures set out by independent bodies, such as the American Architectural Manufacturers Association (AAMA), that, while not governing code, have become industry standard in the United States.[4] |10-13

Form and Fabrication

New digital technologies and complex modeling can consider a greater number of variables and parameters, offering the ability to generate never-before-possible building forms (for example, see SHoP Architects' 290 Mulberry Street project, pp. 132–39). Most important, we now have the ability to model time, evaluating a building not only through the cycle of a day but seasonally as well. Thus, designers have a far greater responsibility to design a fully integrated building by enabling these variable feedback loops from the early stages of the design process onward. This integration can be further enhanced by working directly with manufacturers to achieve the desired design intent without sacrificing performance.

Building information modeling (BIM)—three-dimensional, real-time computer modeling embedded

14 | Burton Place, a residential development in Manchester, England, by Glenn Howells Architects

15 | The effects of weather and time should be positive aspects of a building's design. Burton Place's envelope consists of an arrangement of glass and solid, highly insulated wood panels. The Iroko hardwood used is untreated and is intended to naturally change to a silver color as it ages. In addition to their aesthetic simplicity and structural performance, the materials were all selected with a view to robustness, maintenance, and life span.

with information related to time, space, and specification—is becoming more common and allows for a greater degree of coordination between structure, services, and envelope. It bridges the design, construction, and operation of a building, and since BIM information is consolidated in one data-sharing source, it can reduce the margins of error that occur when separate information sources are used and avoid conflicts that typically wouldn't be apparent until on-site construction. When there is clear communication between the design team, contractor, and fabricators at the initial stages of design, value engineering throughout a project's life span can be integrated as part of a process that all parties have a stake in, rather than becoming a cost-cutting exercise outside of the context of design integration.

Durability

The design life of a building's envelope will be less than that of its structure but greater than that of its internal building systems. For an architect to properly consider the life cycle and maintenance of an envelope's materials, they must create a facade that is accessible and that has the ability to be maintained. Over the life span of a building, parts and assemblies will need to be repaired or replaced: silicon seals will generally last thirty-five years; glass coatings, twenty years; and polyester powder coatings, fifteen years.[5] Durability not only depends on material choice, finish, quality of design, and construction, but also on maintenance and accessibility. Materials and components will not be maintained or replaced if they cannot be accessed by hand or machine, and a well-maintained building will have a longer life span. |14-15

The selection of materials and methods of fabrication for a building envelope are matters of poetic sensibility integrated with pragmatic application. While it needs to be fabricated within given constraints and design parameters and to be able

to withstand wear and tear, an envelope must also bring quality to the internal and external spaces of a building through the perception of the user. These perceptual qualities include how a material interacts with light, how it feels to the touch, and how it weathers over time. |16-18

17| The effects of weathering on a stone and brick wall built around the 1600s in Lavenham, Suffolk, England

18| Texture and play of light on the door of the Sagrada Familia Cathedral in Barcelona, Spain

16| An ivy-clad wall in Lavenham, Suffolk, England

Building Simulation Tools

Edited from text by Matthew Herman, team leader for environmental performance modeling in North America, Buro Happold Consulting Engineers

Climatic data shows us the parameters and extent of the external environment with which the interior of a building needs to operate (see "Climate and Context" in this section, pp. 22–29). It provides the basis for evaluation and testing to find optimum building envelope solutions that are integrated with the overall mass, use, and lifetime performance of a building.

To properly understand any place-specific data, we need to be able to visualize the climatic data and use that information to find opportunities where analysis can be synthesized through design. How does this quantitative data collection change the potential qualitative implications of the internal environment and external appearance through the building envelope? The specifics of climate and the principles of physics form the essential performative basis for a design proposal and its analysis.

Numerous complex variables influence the performance of a building envelope: the dynamic interaction between components, the process of heat transfer, changes in building operational control strategies, user patterns, and climate. All these aspects can quickly overwhelm simplified calculation methods, and they require computers to manage the data. Computational design tools aid in simulating the response of a building to multiple energy flows and their interactions with building components. These tools and the related design process have evolved to be commonly referred to as "building simulation tools."

Zones of Influence
A primary function of a building envelope is to control the transfer of energy between the building's internal environment, as defined by the human body's comfort levels, and the constantly changing external environment. A building envelope's "zone of influence" extends well beyond its immediate thickness, and transfer of energy through the facade is therefore not limited to its composition of materials. This fact is particularly important when considering the environmental performance of any facade design in striving to maintain maximum comfort for building occupants while minimizing energy consumption.

To answer the call for increased performance from a building's envelope as it relates to climate, energy consumption, thermal comfort, and environmental impact, designers must look beyond minimum code standards and rule of thumb design practices. |1 Building simulation tools provide insight and clarity to the often invisible realms of heat, mass, and energy transfer.

The transfer of heat energy through a facade is governed by conduction, convection, and radiation. Radiation and convection are the two processes of heat transfer that heavily influence a facade's

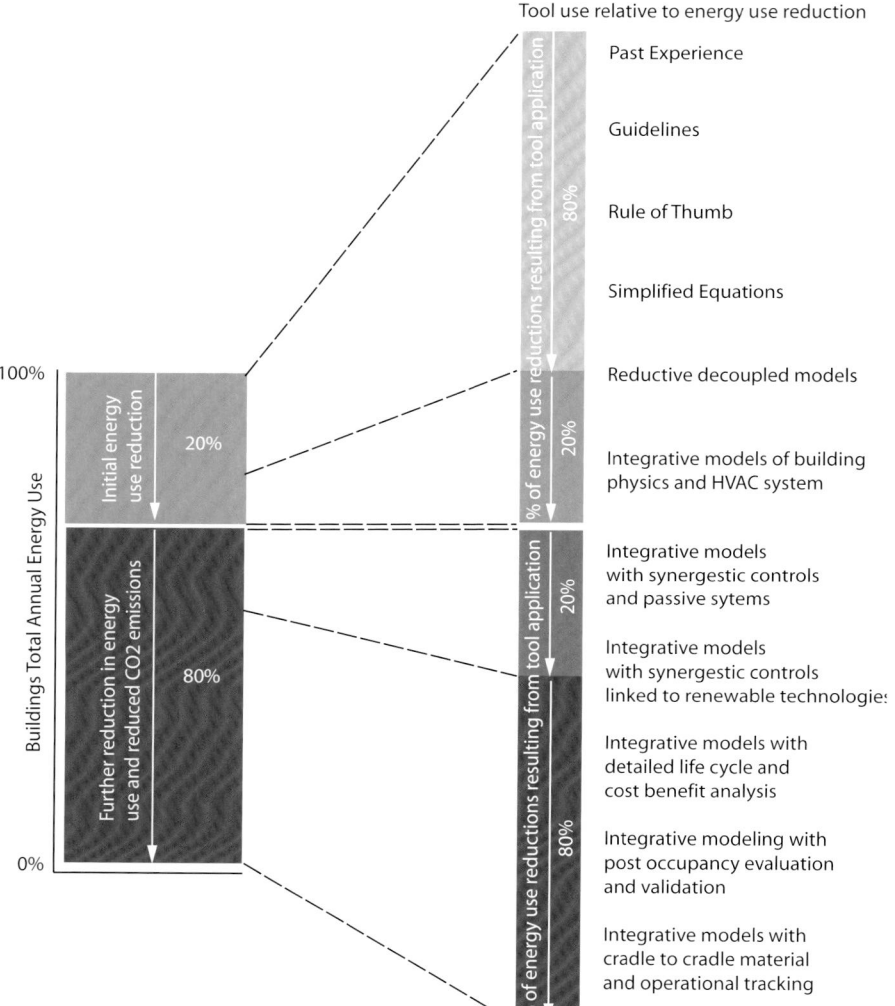

1| This diagram outlines the percentage of potential energy reduction that can be achieved in building design resulting from application of specific tools. The left side indicates the broad "20-80 percent" principle, while the right side zooms in to identify specific applications within the more general percentages. Generally speaking, reductions in annual building energy use can be identified using basic calculations—such as generic rules of thumb or simplified equations—or can be based on past experience and energy guidelines. These methods can target 20 percent energy reduction in building performance. However, through the application of more substantial analysis—such as data interactive computer modeling and post-occupancy feedback loops—a far greater understanding of possible energy and CO_2 reductions can be achieved and implemented by the design team.

performance and extend its zone of influence well beyond its thickness. Only by expanding the area of study beyond a facade's material assembly is it possible to accurately capture the wide variety of climatic and thermodynamic phenomena influencing the facade. This includes transient conduction, surface convection, wind, solar radiation (long wave and short wave), shading and insolation, air flow (wind, pressure, and buoyancy/stack effect), thermal mass, HVAC (heating, ventilation, and air

Model Domain

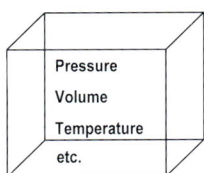

Model State

Change in State

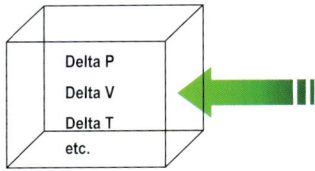

2| A model domain is a space that contains a quantity of matter whose behavior is being investigated. This matter is separated from its surroundings by a boundary that may be physical, such as walls, or simply implied, such as a volume of space. Analysis is based on mass and energy flows across this boundary, for example: delta P (change in pressure), delta V (change in velocity), and delta T (change in temperature).

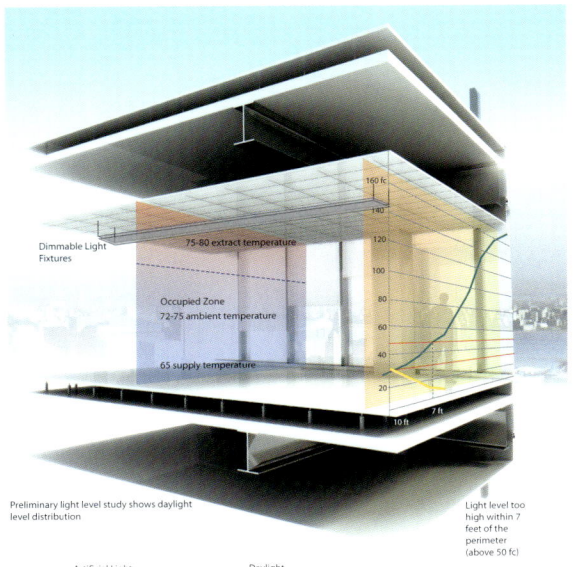

3| A building daylight analysis from Buro Happold Consulting Engineers assesses daylight level drop-offs from the perimeter of an office space and the integration required with artificial lighting levels.

conditioning) systems and controls, internal thermal gains, moisture, and user occupancy patterns.

Model Domain

Environmental building simulation consists of mathematical equations to represent heat-transfer process in relation to mass and energy transfer across a defined area of study. The total number of discrete elements of the building to be studied and the related calculations define the "model domain." |2 The model domain has a set of defined variables—such as pressure, temperature, and material properties of building elements—that require inputs to establish the initial state of the domain and are specified by the designer. The model domain is also defined by geometric and mathematical boundaries that correspond to the limit of the building. Variables and space outside of the boundaries must be input by the model user and may include weather, geospatial coordinates, and fuel types.

Simulation Tools

Three types of related equation sets have been developed in computational engines and software tools: dynamic thermal modeling, computational fluid dynamics, and light simulation. The evolution of these tools is not specific to facades, however the physical phenomena they simulate allows for the accurate modeling of complex mass and energy flows, their interaction with space, and thus the design of envelope. These tools can provide insight into the invisible physics that dictate how a building envelope will perform and how its design will impact building occupants and components within the zone of influence. |3

A dynamic thermal model is the mathematical representation of heat-transfer processes occurring in and around a building. Within a dynamic thermal model conduction, convection, and radiation

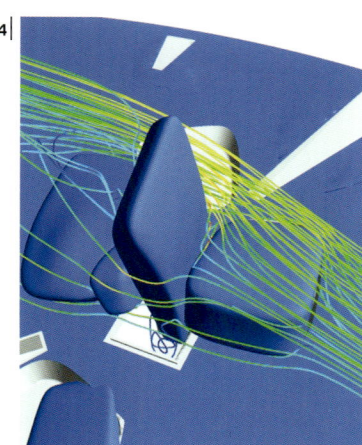

4-6| Engineers at Buro Happold used computational fluid dynamics (CFD) to study airflow patterns for the King Abdulaziz Center for Knowledge and Culture in Saudi Arabia, designed by Snøhetta. The site's destructive desert winds, strong enough to blow surrounding sand and small stones onto the exposed surfaces of the building, drove this specific set of CFD analyses. Lines indicate the flow of wind around the building form, and their varying colors indicate wind speed, with the yellow lines representing the highest wind speeds.

heat-transfer processes are individually modeled for each component of a building envelope and integrated with models of room heat gains, air exchanges, and the HVAC system. The simulation is linked to inputs provided by hourly weather data, allowing it to provide data over a period ranging from a day to a year. The model executes the various heat-transfer calculations for each time step in the model. Outputs from these models tend to be tabular data visualized as charts or graphs showing various time periods or cumulative totals.

When dynamic thermal models and air flow models do not provide sufficient detail or resolution to the physical phenomena being studied, it is necessary to select other computational simulation techniques to provide insight to the environmental performance of the facade, zones of influence, and related spaces and systems. Computational fluid dynamics (CFD) and lighting simulation are often utilized to study more detailed environmental performance issues. |4-6

CFD is a branch of fluid mechanics that utilizes numerical methods to predict fluid flow. These methods require millions of calculations to be performed. When applied to buildings, CFD is often used to understand air flow and heat-transfer processes occurring within and around building spaces given specified boundary conditions, including effects of climate, internal energy sources, and HVAC systems. CFD simulations of air flow and heat-transfer processes are computationally intensive, and may take several hours or days to complete. As such, their use in the design process is typically applied to single instances in time rather than over a longer, dynamic time period, as found in dynamic thermal models. Often, extreme (peak or minimum) times and conditions (as identified in the dynamic thermal model) define the CFD model domain, providing detailed insight into the subtle thermal gradients in a facade and modeling

7|

8|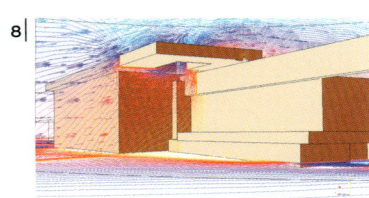

9|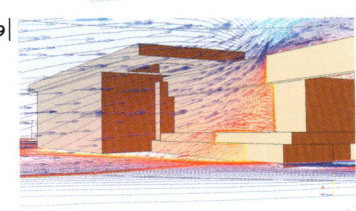

7-9| Architects Westlake Reed Leskosky and consulting engineers Buro Happold used CFD modeling to analyze the form of Hillcrest Hospital in Cleveland, Ohio, at its entry threshold as part of a wind-mitigation strategy for user comfort and safety. Figures 8 and 9 show perspective-view studies of wind speeds around an entry, while figure 7 shows the same studies in plan view, but of the larger area around the site as well. The orange to blue color scale indicates wind speed, from low to high.

the velocity and temperature of air flow through openings and into adjoining spaces. |**7-9**

Lighting simulations used in the design of a building envelope typically address daylight quality and distribution issues within the zone of influence. Lighting calculations require detailed descriptions of surface properties and light sources. In facade design, the description of the glass and interior surfaces and finishes are critical to the quality of the results. When doing daylight analysis it is also necessary to understand the various sky models that describe the location and distribution of sunlight within the model domain.

Reading Output

Simulation tools are just that: tools. A designer must be able to take building simulation output and know how to use the information to work toward a solution to a specific design problem. To do this, it is important to frame analysis goals governed by a rigorous structure. A baseline needs to be established beforehand against which outcomes can be measured and assessed. |**10** This process is increasingly important as the building envelope is recognized as a zone where real impact can be made in overall reduction of energy use and carbon dioxide emissions. Developments in software (such as Ecotect and Radiance) are enabling a far more visual discussion between architects and engineers and a real, productive feedback loop, especially during the planning, programming, and schematic design stages.

Feedback Loops of Form and Performance   47

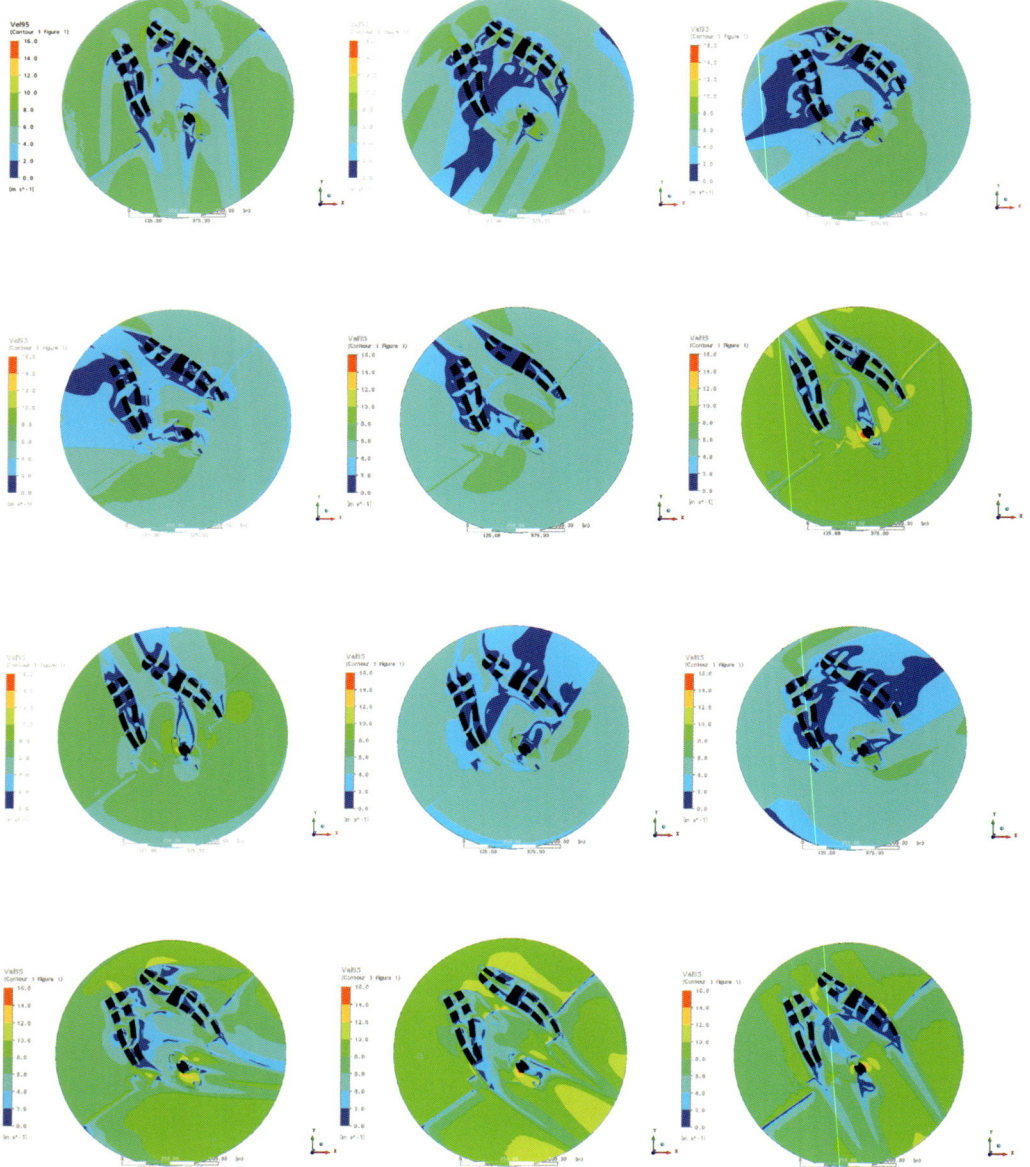

10 | Buro Happold created these plan-view airflow study patterns for the King Abdulaziz Center for Knowledge and Culture in Saudi Arabia. In the diagrams, red indicates the highest wind speeds and dark blue indicates the lowest wind speeds.

Life Cycle Analysis

How do we bring long-term value into the design of building envelopes? |1 A building's envelope is both a big-ticket item of initial capital expenditure (15 to 35 percent of its construction cost) and also has a major impact on the performance and users of the building. When thoughtfully integrated with structure and systems, a building's envelope has an enormous potential to bring increased value to a project, and not necessarily at a premium cost.

Life cycle, as the term implies, considers the whole life of a building, not just the initial project

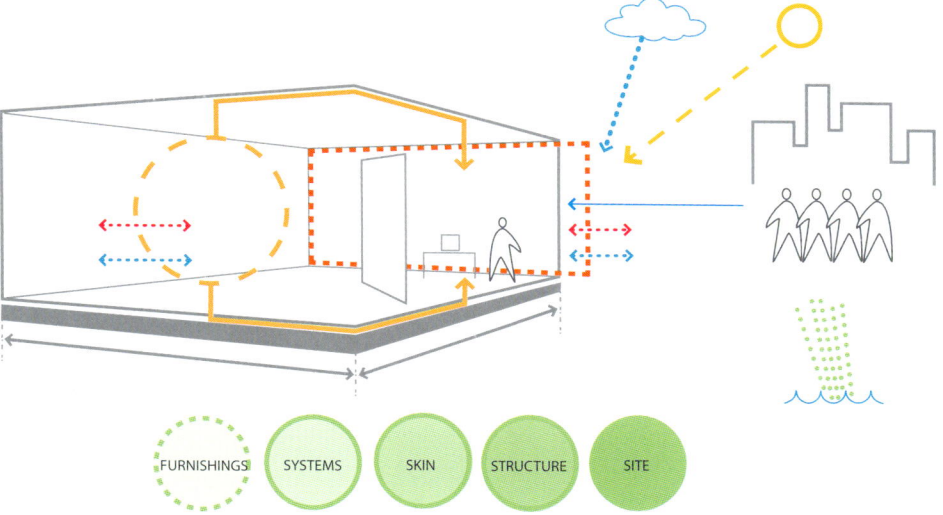

1| This diagram, developed from Stewart Brand's book *How Buildings Learn*, identifies elements of a building relative to their "turnover," or life cycle. The site is the most permanent aspect of a building, with an expected life span of thirty to three hundred years. A building's envelope has an expected life span of twenty to twenty-five years. The life span of services systems depends on the technologies employed and how embedded they are within the building fabric. The elements with the fastest turnover are those that relate to space planning and furnishings. The intent, performance, buildability, procurement, and cost of a building's envelope all play a part in the lifetime value of a building. This diagram shows the envelope (the dashed orange zone) as central to these components, relating to the interior conditions of services (distribution shown with the dashed yellow circle and solid arrows) and furnishings/space planning, as well as to the exterior site conditions, including context, location, and climate.

and construction costs. Gary Lawrence, an Urban Strategies leader for Arup, believes that the value designers and consultants can bring to a project is not solely a monetary one, but includes a sense of comfort, security, and overall spatial quality.[1] While at some point value does need to be defined in financial terms, there are many decisions that have to be made that are not easy to put a specific cost to, such as the overall environmental impact of a building. Responsibility for value does not rest solely at the door of the client or the design team, but it does start there. The degree of building users' collective responsibility is manifest through the design team's response to the client's brief. In the case of sealed buildings, users have no opportunity for responsibility, whereas a naturally ventilated building is likely to require user participation. This responsibility has to be communicated during initial discussions with the client and ultimately through clear, ongoing communications with building's operation management of how to use the building for optimum performance.

Five Parameters of Value
Davis Langdon LLP, international construction and cost consultants, have suggested five intrinsic parameters of envelope design strategy in relation to value: intent, performance, buildability, procurement, and cost.[2] All five issues relate to the initial brief as set out by the client, and are described below.

A project's intent outlines requirements (usually set by the client) such as square footage, building function, and whether it is to meet specific environmental reference standards such as LEED (Leadership in Energy and Environmental Design, U.S. Green Building Council) or BREEAM (Building Research Establishment Environmental Assessment Method, in the United Kingdom). As the design team progresses, these client requirements will be expanded to become the architectural intent of the project, addressing other issues such as site and context.

In terms of building envelope design, performance describes functions in response to climate, water, heat, light, air, and energy. Generally these issues are governed by code, but depending on the intent of the client and team, performance may be expected to go above and beyond legislation. Each aspect of performance is invariably related to others: air permeability relates to heat gain and loss but must also address condensation. Maximization of daylight must be balanced with potential solar heat gain to reduce the need for artificial light without

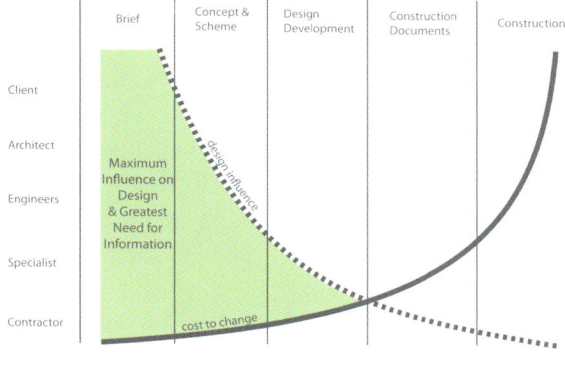

2| This graph shows a traditional procurement route, where the client approaches an architect, the design team is formed, specialists are consulted, the project goes out to bid, and a contractor is hired. The chart makes clear that the most fruitful dialogue with the contractor would happen at the front end of the design process, where the greatest need for information aligns with the maximum influence of the design team. Design changes made late in the building's design development process are much more costly.

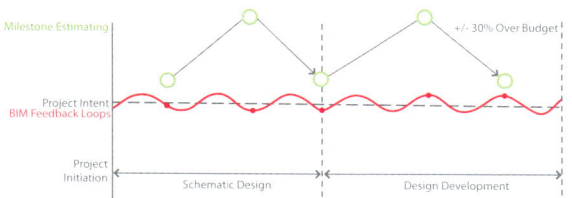

3| This diagram shows how building information modeling (BIM) allows for information feedback loops between the design team members—and potentially the contractor—during the design process, enabling a more integrated design response. As a result of the close relationship between design, specification, and cost in a BIM model, it is possible to review cost in relation to intent as part of a more frequent process—shown here by arrows moving from the milestone estimation points (green circles) back in line with the project's intent.

increasing cooling requirements. Every issue related to performance has a direct impact on intent.

Value in terms of buildability means ensuring that the design intent and performance criteria can be built efficiently using a number of sources and that the sequences of fabrication, transportation, installation, and maintenance are thoroughly considered. For example, if large panels of glazing are proposed as part of the building envelope, these will need to be fabricated and assembled, transported and installed, and potentially replaced in a safe and efficient manner with minimal disruption. It is the responsibility of the team to ensure that a building's components can be built, maintained, and replaced over its life—if a building has a fifty-year design life and the building envelope has a twenty-five-year design life, access to the envelope for repairs and/or maintenance must be considered in the initial design strategy.

The procurement of a building envelope fundamentally relates to whether or not it can be bought and delivered at the expected quality and within the time frame of the project intent. Two key components of procurement are avoiding single sourcing—i.e., having the option to approach a number of suppliers, fabricators, and contractors—and secondly, to have early engagement with all of an envelope's sources—building envelopes take a relatively long time to design, source, and manufacture, so if a design team positively engages with sources earlier in the design process, there is a far greater potential to achieve integrated solutions. |2-3

The final issue relating to value in building envelope design is cost. Ultimately, there is a capital cost for everything, and this must align with the client's intent and budget. Intent, performance, buildability, procurement, and cost are all intrinsic to value, and for a fully integrated building envelope to be realized, these issues have to relate to the whole life of the building.

Whole-Life Adaptability

It is important to consider flexibility, potential change of use, and context as part of an envelope's whole-life value. For example, the cost of including operable windows or vents in the envelope of a building on a noisy, busy street today could be worth it over the life of the building. Not only is the energy needed for mechanical systems likely to get more expensive, but over the next few years shifting trends in transportation could considerably lower noise pollution in urban areas. As technology improves and traffic noise and emissions are reduced over the next, say, ten years of the twenty-five-year life of an urban building envelope, windows could be operable for the subsequent fifteen years—the original barrier to natural ventilation (depending on climate) having changed over time. The effects of changing conditions and context over time must be considered as part of the design intent.

Life Cycle

The expected life span of a building is an important factor of intent, and it determines the required durability of a building envelope. Life cycle can be considered from the aspect of environmental impact as well as in terms of financial return on investment. Life cycle assessment (LCA) is a technique used to assess the environmental aspects and potential impacts associated with a product, process, or service, by first compiling an inventory of relevant energy and material inputs and environmental emissions and then evaluating the potential environmental impacts associated with these identified inputs and releases.[3] Life cycle cost analysis (LCCA), or whole-life cost, is an "economic method of project evaluation in which all costs arising from owing, operating, maintaining, and ultimately dismantling a project are considered to be potentially important."[4] Life cycle assessment and life cycle cost analysis, while related, are different issues.

The tools for measuring both LCA and LCCA are complex, but industry standards continue to be put in place and software calculation tools are becoming more sophisticated to allow for comparison and benchmarking of combined monetary and environmental costs, related both to specific design decisions and across projects for the construction, maintenance, replacement, and, ultimately, recycling of a building.[5] A calculation of the embodied energy of the constituent parts of a building envelope is possible, but a view of the whole integrated assembly gives a greater environmental picture than the consideration of separate components. Ultimately, the performance of an appropriate, well-made facade fabricated more than five hundred miles off-site is better than a poorly built, underperforming facade made locally. Simple payback analysis is sometimes not enough to fully realize the advantages of integration of form and performance. The benefits of the whole must be measured against intent, so that a project's value engineering is a constant process, not a post-rationalized, false analysis.

Over thirty years of a building's life, its operations and utilities will cost nearly as much as its initial construction.[6] Quality of space related to occupation is subjective and hard to measure, but people over time cost more than construction. Salary costs alone can be nearly three times the cost of physically housing employees in an office building (including lease, mortgage, utilities, and facilities-management costs) over a single year.[7] In order for a building to be sustainable, its initial intent must account for the comfort of its users over time. In terms of the building envelope, this includes how the threshold between inside and outside is controlled and adapted and the quality of the environment it provides. The key to understanding long-term value for building envelope design is in the durability and adaptability of form and performance.

Section II: Elements of a Holistic Approach

Internal and external environments are not completely divided by a building envelope: they perpetually overlap through a series of layers, cycles, and systems. Rather than thinking of the issues that a building envelope has to address as problems of mitigation, they should be considered as possibilities for integration—the coordinated response to the issues of air, structure, and light in buildings through a design strategy.

Over the past one hundred years, the design of a typical building envelope has radically changed from a monolithic mass to a series of layers, each with a specific, pragmatic task. In addition to offering an external and internal face to the building, these layers need to repel rainwater, control water vapor, retain heat or coolness, and handle air transmission. These layers also tend to be more lightweight and, rather than relying on building mass to insulate, employ a supplemental insulation layer when climate requires it.

While envelope designs have become far more sophisticated and varied, there are two problems related to the performance of their lighter layers, specifically in temperate climates. The first is that thermal lag is greatly reduced due to their decreased mass, so internal temperatures fluctuate more quickly through the envelope, resulting in increased peak loads, which dictate the size of mechanical systems and distribution. The second is that the insulation layer can easily be compromised by any building element bridging it. When structure or substructure penetrates this layer, it is likely to transfer cold from outside to inside (usually), creating condensation between the layers that can eventually cause corrosion, dry rot, and mold growth. The solution to these problems is to use an integrated design strategy as a coordinated response to the issues of structure, materials, assembly, and environment in buildings.

When teaching basic construction courses, I have used the following example to bring home the importance of integrating pragmatic issues and poetic sensibility when designing: A series of building details are presented—specifically of where the envelope meets the ground—to show that all meet the technical needs of any given situation. They transfer and resist load from the superstructure (aboveground) and substructure (belowground), withstand and resist water in all forms (vapor, liquid, and solid), and help retain temperature (hot or cold) in the internal environment. However, there is an additional obligation of these combined components—to reflect an aesthetic sensibility for the delight of users, while also meeting pragmatic requirements. This is what makes a building into architecture.

In what I have defined as the "push me-pull you" principle, good design requires a truly holistic approach in terms of form and performance. All components of assemblies and systems should work together. If you change or develop a technical aspect, an aesthetic detail, or the "cost" of an element, everything else must be considered and reconsidered in a continuous loop of development. A building's envelope is a complex, interconnected mesh, but the best and simplest outcomes develop from a real and invested understanding of the envelope at every scale, and are materialized through elegant solutions.

While separated in this section for clarification, the elements of air, heat, water, materials, light, and energy completely and invariably coexist with each other and cannot be considered in isolation. If you change a design on the basis of the push me-pull you principle, no element can be transformed without reviewing the impact upon all the other elements. The following parts of this section are all structured under four headings: problems, principles, potential, and possibility. "Problems" briefly outlines existing conditions to be recognized and challenged, while "principles" takes us back to the foundational basic truths of performance and implication in relation to the building envelope. "Potential" directs a path that we could take at little or no cost but with great benefit in shifting from a "business as usual" stance, while "possibility" identifies just the tip of the iceberg of contemporary research, where collective innovation could make a real impact on the future building envelope design.

Problems

There are obstacles that must be overcome if we are going to get an integrated building envelope strategy right, and it is important to recognize them even at a basic level. Not all these issues are specifically related to building envelopes, and while some can readily be defined—such as materials, assembly methods, legislation, and economics—others are less tangible—such as aesthetics, light quality, and social expectations. Some problems are the result of the status quo, and accepted norms need to be reviewed systematically; others need to be balanced with the dynamic nature of context.

Principles

To reconceive a problem as a possibility, the principles of its situation must be understood. In the case of building envelopes, this requires looking at the interactions between layers of materials, assemblies, and systems within the contexts of place, program, and occupation. Good design requires the pragmatic dissection and optimization of the different variables between principles and specifics.

Potential

Modern facade design is about opportunities: exploiting positives, not cancelling negatives.[1] Potential comes from recognizing possibility in problems through an integrated overview, not from seeking resolution in a piecemeal fashion.

Possibility

If we slightly alter our perception of the term *element*, there is actually just one element that architects need to address: carbon. Buildings will always require resources and energy, but the goal of design and renovation must be to minimize carbon emissions as much as possible. A building's envelope must have optimal environmental controls and function as a potentially productive surface (whether vertical or horizontal) that can actually contribute to the world's energy resources rather than just deplete them. It is too easy to either take a dismissive stance toward or be overly consumed with a "sustainable" agenda—it is not an either/or status. Rather, it is the environmental glue that holds the design process together. Sustainability is just what we should strive for as designers and architects, and as such, it should be a consideration in every aspect of design.

Sustainability cannot be an ex post facto addition to a building. Each potential in the following sections outlines just one of many ways that research into the components, assemblies, and systems of building envelopes could create a paradigm shift in the conception of enclosure, becoming truly multifunctional.

Air:
Flow and Ventilation

Wind and air movement on the surface of a building generate differential pressures that drive air through gaps and openings, intentionally or otherwise, to ventilate a building. Depending on the varied and dynamic conditions of the external environment, climate, and the requirements of internal space, a building's envelope is the surface area through which ventilation can occur, and it must always act as a barrier to unwanted air leakage.

Air: Problems |1

Often, architects who don't have a true understanding of how air movement occurs draw obedient airflow arrows that do not convey the dynamic process of air movement on building section drawings. Fresh air is assumed (or denied), and a constant internal building temperature is accepted and endured—regardless of the external environment. We have come to expect stability through forced-air systems since so many buildings now operate this way. Many of us even keep a cardigan or jacket on the back of our chair because we know the building we work in is likely to be too cold even in mid-summer, and we are frustrated by sealed windows on sunny, temperate days. User expectations are defined by a culture of mechanically controlled internal environments: this is a manufactured sense of comfort.

Many buildings are mechanically air-conditioned or ventilated to control air-change rates, humidity, and temperature, and to exhaust contaminants and dilute indoor air with outdoor air. For systems efficiency, buildings are often sealed up to stop imbalances in the system through user interaction—for example, the opening of windows.

Materials used to line ceilings, walls, and floors, and in furniture fabrication, can seriously affect indoor air quality. These are the components of a building that are replaced most frequently and can be the most toxic to internal air quality. Sick building

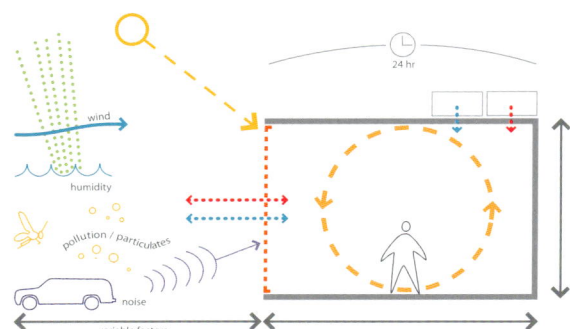

1| Air: problems
This diagram articulates the problems related to air that need to be addressed by the building envelope: the variable factors of the outside condition—climate, orientation, adjacencies (such as traffic), and time (day/night/season)—together with the expectations of the interior condition—building size (height and depth), program, systems integration, and user expectation. We have come to expect a constant internal condition that can be provided by air conditioning.

syndrome (SBS)—where building occupants experience acute health and comfort effects that appear to be linked to time spent in a building, but no specific illness or cause can be identified—is attributed mostly to poor indoor-air quality, related in part to problems with heating, ventilation, and air-conditioning (HVAC) systems.[1] Studies have shown that fully air-conditioned systems have the highest occurrence of SBS in occupants. Additionally, individuals lose contact with, and connection to, their external environment and have little or no control over their internal environment in sealed buildings.

Most mechanical systems in the United States are forced-air systems, where supply-and-return air ducts are located in the ceiling zone and drop cold air down at the perimeter of the building to counter heat gain through the building envelope and internal zones. This can cause discomfort in supply areas, increases floor-to-floor heights (and therefore area and cost of the envelope), and supplies controlled air at the furthest point from users, i.e., at the ceiling rather than the floor.

Simply adding operable windows is not necessarily the answer. Incorrectly orientated, planned, and sized openings can cause other problems to arise. Ventilation rates (air changes per hour in a space) can become inconstant and unreliable. Drafts can cause discomfort, and noise pollution can make it hard to concentrate. Lack of coordination with building systems can lead to energy waste. Internal planning and potential future use of space can be compromised by furniture and partition layouts that prevent window operation and disrupt potential cross ventilation.

Building systems labor to maintain temperatures within a lightweight envelope, but the air barrier of a wall assembly can often be compromised (especially at junctions with openings). Any air leakage out through the external envelope takes with it conditioned air at an energy cost, since we are

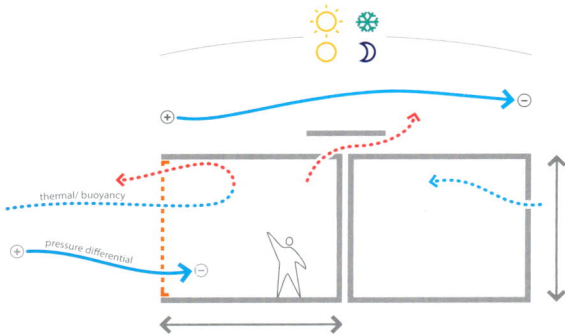

2 | Air: principles
Air movement is driven by pressure differential and thermal buoyancy. Air flow will always be from an area of positive pressure to negative, or from hot to cold. This can be utilized in building envelope and systems integration through consideration of the depth and height of the building/space and the location and size of openings, whether in the vertical building envelope (facade) or the horizontal (roof). Consideration will depend on location, orientation, time of day, and seasonal temperature variables.

For figures 3 to 6: In Sauerbruch Hutton's Jessop West building—built in 2008 in Sheffield, England, with RMJM—the principle of stack effect is utilized to integrate an air supply-and-extraction system into the building envelope, enabling natural ventilation and operable windows, even adjacent to heavy road traffic. The air intake is decoupled from the operable windows to allow noise to be attenuated before it reaches the interior. Exhaust air is then drawn by stack effect through a vent in the window jamb, up a chimney zone, and to roof-level vents.

3 | External context photograph of Jessop West

then effectively heating or cooling the outside. Air infiltration and exfiltration are the major sources of energy inefficiency in building envelopes.

Air: Principles |2

In building envelope design, air should be considered in relation to two broad issues: air exchange for ventilation and air barriers in the wall assembly that prevent loss of heated or chilled air to the exterior.

Internal airflow can be altered by creating a pressure differential using thermal buoyancy, where less-dense hot air rises and more-dense cold air is drawn in to replace the displaced hot air—this is also called the "stack effect." This basic principle can be applied to building envelope design both at the scale of the wall assembly and at the scale of the whole building section in order to take advantage of natural ventilation.

In principle, air will move from a positive pressure zone to a negative pressure zone, always trying to create equilibrium through pressure differential. At the scale of the whole building, wind velocity and direction must also be taken into account. There will be positive pressure on the windward side of a building, but this is not constant and depends on specific site and seasonal variations. If air changes are dependent on direction, the worst-case scenario should be taken into account—the leeward side of a building (farthest from the pressure-driven side). The overall height of a building and adjacent buildings and landscape can significantly change airflows, as will the area, orientation, and profile of the building envelope.

In a double-skin envelope, where an interstitial air pocket is created between two layers of materials—typically glass—the stack effect is driven by solar heat gain. As air between the double skin heats up, it rises, drawing in cooler air from below. This principle is based on thermal air buoyancy, and can be applied at the scale of one window unit, a whole

4| Detail photograph showing the solar air flues and windows of Jessop West's building envelope

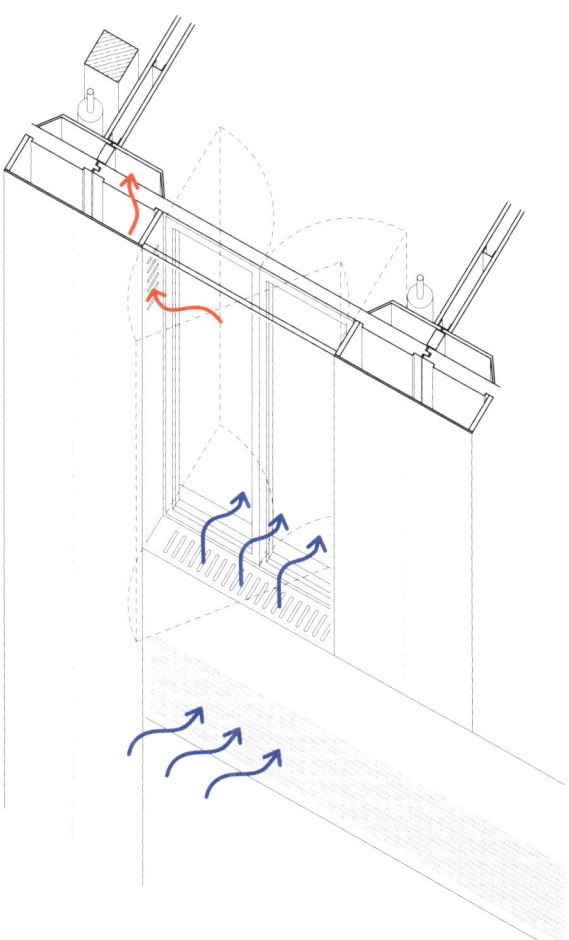

5| Detail photograph showing the vent in the window jamb: This vent allows exhaust air to be drawn up the solar flues by the stack effect.

6| This diagram shows the integration of window, venting, and solar flues for Jessop West. Incoming air (blue) is drawn in through the attenuator under the window to a vent between the outer and inner window units, where it can either be allowed into the occupied room by opening the inner window or utilized to draw heat up through the chimney through stack effect (red).

Elements of a Holistic Approach

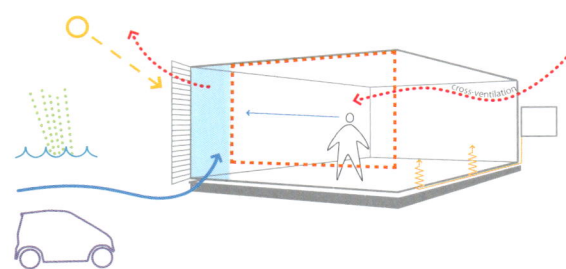

7 | Air: potential
A building's envelope should be an active component of any ventilation strategy. Through careful consideration of context and climate, the facade can maximize the potential of passive ventilation, eliminating or reducing dependence on active systems. It is also likely that, as other technologies develop, issues related to noise and pollution will be reconsidered. For example, if more cars become electrically powered over the next decade, noise and pollution considerations for building envelopes addressing urban street conditions would dramatically shift.

wall, or a building section with a central courtyard or atrium space in order to exhaust air and heat from a space through the envelope. |3-6

An air barrier in a wall section is dependent on continuity. Any failure or disruption in this continuity will cause an air pressure differential, leading to the passage of air, and potentially water vapor, through the assembly. Careful consideration and coordination of detailing—especially between systems—and good-quality construction will help ensure that a building envelope acts as a contiguous air barrier. Air leakage should be tested once construction is complete. This test is done by pressurizing the entire interior of a building with a fan and measuring the time it takes for that pressure to equalize.

Air: Potential |7
To maximize the potential of a well-integrated building envelope, architects and engineers must start planning and coordinating early in the design process. This requires that the building envelope be considered as an active component of the ventilation system for the whole building and that it be coordinated with the structural strategy from the outset of the design process.

As mechanical ventilation systems have developed, a greater number of deep-plan buildings have been built. Less than one hundred years ago, building plans were typically not as deep and had greater operable window-to-plan area ratios to take advantage of daylight and cross ventilation. As a rule of thumb, single-sided ventilation will suit a plan of up to twenty feet deep; double sided, forty feet deep. This is without a central atrium core zone, which would enable potential greater plan depth.

An intermediate microclimate zone can be utilized to introduce cool, fresh air into a building and provide gathering areas for users. In tall buildings these zones are often called "sky gardens," but the

8 | View of the central atrium, Federal Environment Agency, Sauerbruch Hutton, Dessau, Germany, 2005

9| Office windows opening onto the central atrium, Federal Environment Agency, Sauerbruch Hutton, Dessau, Germany, 2005

10| View of the external building envelope with air intake vents, Federal Environment Agency, Sauerbruch Hutton, Dessau, Germany, 2005

same principle can be seen in low-rise buildings. For example, architecture firm Sauerbruch Hutton's Federal Environment Agency building in Dessau, Germany, not only has a narrow plan allowing for cross ventilation through offices, but also includes a central courtyard as a non-conditioned buffer zone. |8-10

Mixed-mode systems employ a combination of natural and mechanical ventilation systems. When external conditions are favorable, windows can be opened for ventilation, and air-conditioning is used only as needed—when external conditions are too hot, humid, or noisy, or when there are infrequent additional heat loads such as more people than usual in a meeting space. This combined system can be coordinated through sensors feeding information to a building management system (BMS) or have user overrides for direct control. A study by the Center for the Built Environment (CBE) states that "research has found that building occupants prefer a wider range of indoor thermal conditions when they are provided with some measure of personal control,"[2] and energy consumption can be greatly reduced by only relying on mechanical systems when really needed. For example, in St. Louis, Missouri, most buildings are mechanically conditioned, but for approximately two-thirds of the year external conditions are sufficiently favorable to allow for natural ventilation if the building envelope is managed correctly.

Airflow depends on design factors, location, time of day, and season. We expect windows to be a source of both daylight and air. Decoupling or reconfiguring air intake and extraction from visual contact and view can allow greater control of airflow through a building's envelope (as in the Sauerbruch Hutton buildings described in this section). Strategies such as nighttime cooling of a space through the opening of windows need building envelopes that incorporate insect and rain screens, security measures,

Elements of a Holistic Approach   65

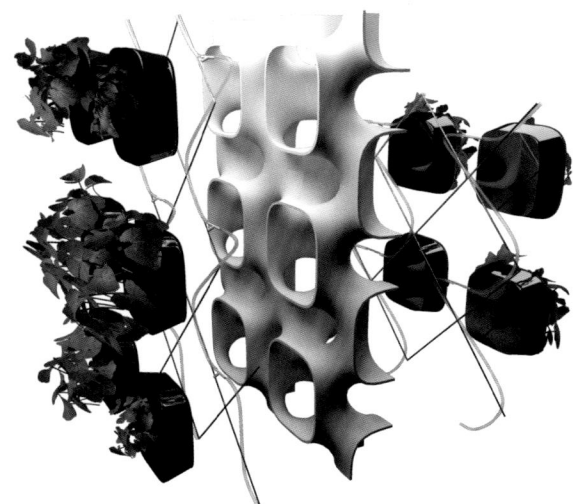

11| A diagram of the Active Phytoremediation System (APS), developed by the Center for Architecture Science and Ecology (CASE) at Rensselaer Polytechnic Institute, shows its central air plenum and modular inserts of plant material.

and robust mechanisms, but they also fundamentally need to be operated effectively, which requires the education of building users well beyond initial design and construction.

Air: Possibility |11

The Active Phytoremediation System (APS), developed by the Center for Architecture Science and Ecology (CASE) at Rensselaer Polytechnic Institute, is a biomechanical hybrid system that improves indoor air quality while decreasing both the energy consumption and exposure to external air pollution associated with conventional air-conditioning systems.[3] The APS operates by amplifying the air-cleaning capacity of common plants by over two hundred times. It does this by actively drawing air from within the building through the roots and rhizomes of the plants, where pollutants are then trapped and digested within the system before the air is redistributed to occupied spaces. The APS is composed of optimized modules that house a variety of plant types in hydroponic cartridges.

Due to its modularity, the system is highly scalable, and it could be architecturally integrated into a wide range of building sizes and typologies. The module is a product designed for disassembly and recycling that capitalizes on low-cost, high-tech emerging manufacturing techniques to improve the potential for adaptable reuse in multiple architectural applications.

The APS is targeted to reduce a significant number of health risks associated with SBS through actively removing volatile organic compounds (VOCs), particulate matter, and other biological and chemical pollutants from internal air, while introducing humidity to heated interiors during the cold season. It also dramatically lowers a building's overall energy consumption by reducing the need for fresh-air intake while also limiting exposure to external urban-air pollutants, such as ozone.

Heat:
Gain and Loss

Just as our skin is a zone of thermal exchange for our bodies, so too is an envelope for a building. Cooling and space heating accounts for approximately 50 percent of energy use in commercial buildings in the United States and internal environmental systems invariably operate in spite of, rather than assisted by, building envelope performance.

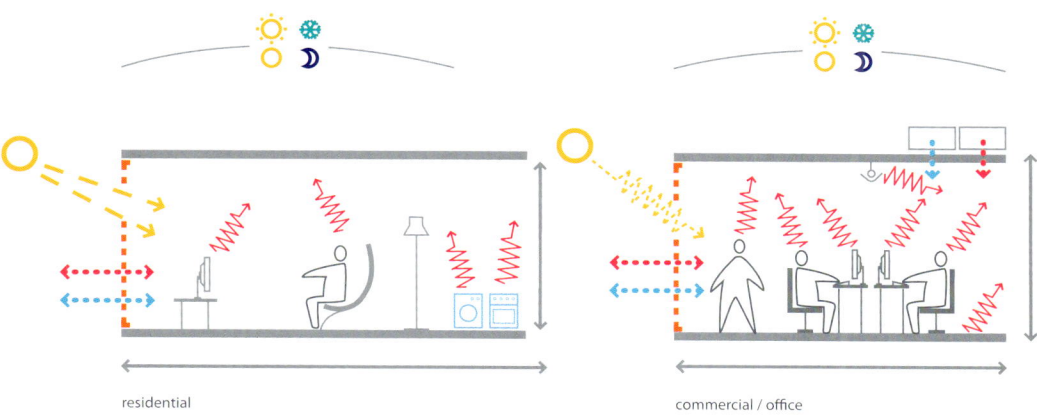

residential   commercial / office

1| Heat: problems
This diagram identifies the differences associated with heat for residential buildings (left) and commercial/office buildings (right). Both are dependent on the time of day and season as well as building construction type, floor-to-floor height, and plan depth. However, office spaces are likely to have more occupants as well as equipment, and will therefore need to address heat gain (especially in the afternoons) as a primary concern.

Heat: Problems |1
Modern building envelopes, enabled by steel and concrete-frame construction, are lightweight and incorporate large areas of glazing. Compared with load-bearing masonry walls, unitized and curtain wall systems have a low thermal-storage capacity and rely on layers of insulation or glass to resist heat loss.

    Our building envelopes are leaky, and they too freely transfer hot or cold air to the external environment, wasting energy. Inconsistent air barriers, untested for air leakage levels, are a high source of energy waste in buildings. Large expanses of poorly specified glass will transfer solar heat gain to the interior of a building, while badly detailed and constructed walls will transfer heat to a cold exterior. Building codes are based on meeting specified minimums on paper, instead of on-site testing. Buildings are not required to meet maximum best-practice performance through integrated systems.

Elements of a Holistic Approach

The desire for transparency in our buildings has been aligned with the area of glazing often used in them, but 100 percent glazing is not required in order to achieve sufficient daylight levels (see "Daylighting: Comfort and Control," pp. 83-88), and brings with it serious challenges from solar heat gain or loss to the outside.

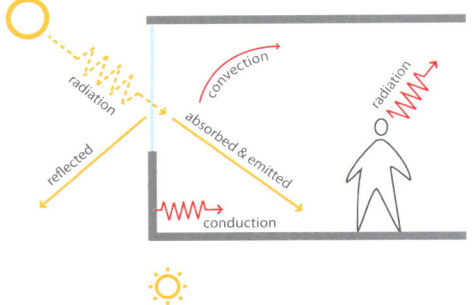

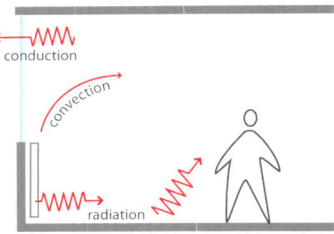

2 | Heat: principles
Heat flow through a building envelope into an enclosed space will vary depending on climate, season, daily high and low temperatures, orientation, and solar exposure. Thermal energy moves from hot to cold though radiation, convection, and/or conduction.

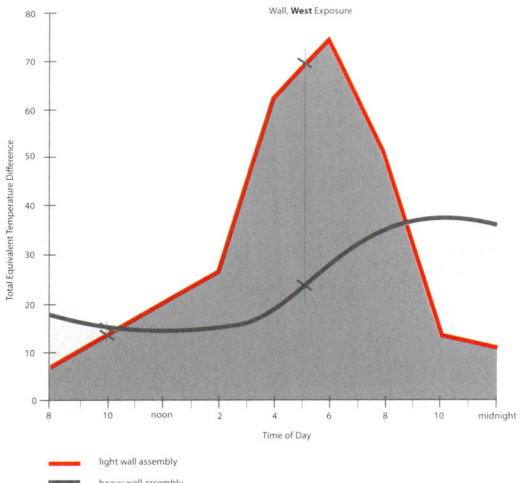

3 | A heat-curve diagram, originally derived from ASHRAE data, indicates the temperature difference through both light and heavy envelopes for a west-facing facade in St. Louis, Missouri. The heavy wall's line indicates how the peak load of the interior has been mitigated, thereby lowering the peak design loads for its building's systems.

Heat: Principles |2
Heat flow is the physical process by which energy moves from a hot zone or body to a cold one through one of three mechanisms: radiation, convection, or conduction. When it is cold outside, internal heat will try to flow out through a building's envelope, and vice versa when it is hot outside.

Internal heat gains depend on the functions, program, and equipment of the space enclosed. External heat gains depend on location in the world (climate and microclimate), solar intensity, and building adjacencies. The combined maximum internal and external heat gains and losses represent a peak loading. It is this peak load against which mechanical systems are designed. If the load can be spread over a period of time, peak loads are reduced and so are mechanical system specifications and, ultimately, energy use. If the peaks and troughs can be reduced or flattened out at points of peak load, less energy will be needed to maintain comfort levels in a building. |3

Mass provides a thermal lag (heat capacity and conductivity over time). Concrete, for example, will

Building Envelopes   68

absorb heat and release it once there is a temperature differential. Provided that the surface is in contact with a space, this principle of thermal lag can be applied both to delay heat transfer, reducing peak loads on a space, and to reuse the absorbed heat or coolness for an overall system advantage.

A material with trapped layers or pockets of air will have a higher resistance to heat loss than a dense material. Therefore, insulation will provide resistance to heat loss through an assembly. A material's U-value (Btu/hr·ft^2·°F) is the rate of heat flow lost through an element or assembly through conduction for a unit of temperature difference—the greater the number, the greater the heat loss. An R-value (ft^2·°F·hr/Btu) indicates the resistance to heat flow by an element or assembly—the greater the number, the greater the resistance (U=1/R).[1]

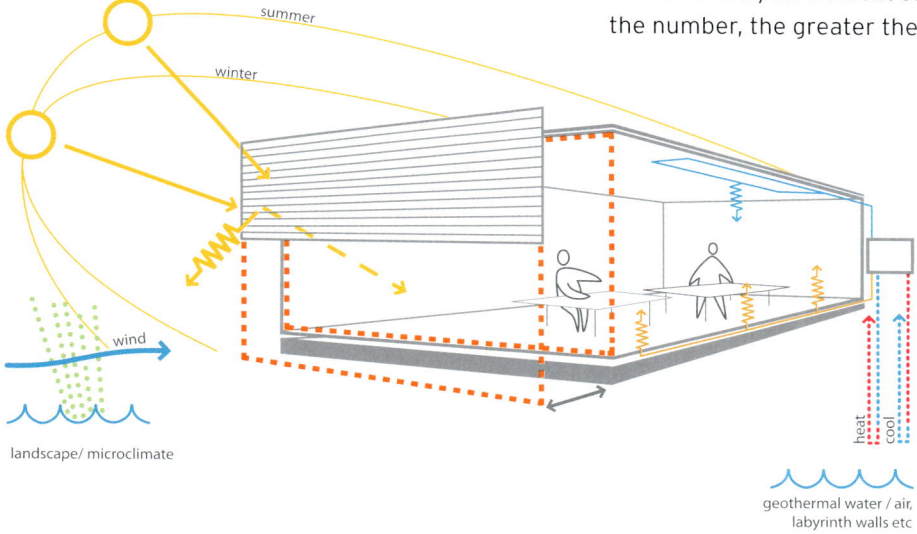

4 | Heat: potential
The depth of a building's envelope and shading devices (as depicted as part of the envelope system on this diagram) can be exploited to address or utilize potential solar heat gain as well as maximize daylighting potential. In addition to direct systems, integrated building envelope design can coordinate with engineered alternative sources of heating and cooling (such as geothermal heating or belowground labyrinth walls to cool intake air), the site's landscape strategy and specific microclimate, and their effect on a building's internal environment as a holistic approach.

Heat: Potential | 4
Wherever possible, a building's orientation should be optimized to reduce or increase solar heat gains as required. East and west elevations are the hardest to control in terms of heat gains, since the sun is at a lower angle of incidence to the building envelope and is at its most variable. Generally, it is recommended that architects design commercial

Elements of a Holistic Approach

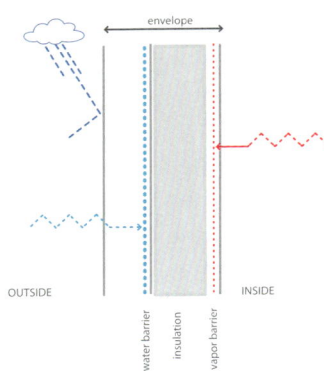

5 | A typical wall assembly, with separate water and vapor barriers

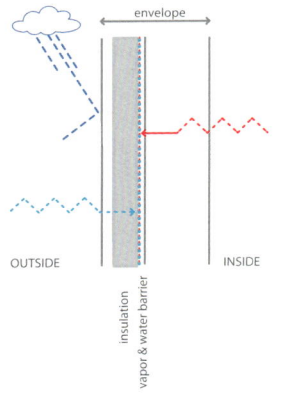

6 | A wall assembly with uninterrupted insulation and combined water and vapor barriers

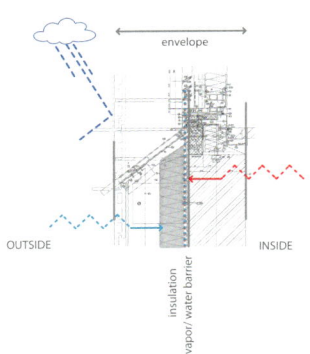

7 | Through the introduction of cast-in-place concrete infill panels, architects Allies and Morrison (with Buro Happold as environmental engineers and Whitbybird as structural engineers) designed the envelope for the Faculty of English building in Cambridge, England (see pp. 116–23), to absorb heat during the day, reducing peak loads on the internal space. The offices are then purged of excess heat through a nighttime natural-ventilation strategy.

buildings with greater north and south areas of envelope where possible, while because of the nature of their occupation, this is not so critical for residential buildings. Early studies can also enable consideration of surface-to-volume ratio and the massing of a building. A good design will control heat gains while allowing daylight to reduce lighting loads.

The integration of a building's envelope with structural and environmental systems offers possibilities such as using the structure as a thermal sink (a mass that absorbs and dissipates heat) to absorb heat gains. A more massive structure, combined with a well-insulated building envelope, will retain stored heat in the winter that can then be radiated back into the space at night, avoiding cold starts in the mornings.

High-performance glazing (with low U-values), good thermal performance of solid or opaque areas of the envelope, and continuity of the air barrier are essential to maximizing the performance of a building's envelope in terms of energy performance. Air leakage tests carried out during the commissioning of a building offer a check for overall air-barrier performance and identify points of failure.

The performance of an assembly must not be negatively affected by cold bridging. Good insulation only insulates if it is not compromised by parts of the assembly—for example, metal studs—transferring cold through it. If insulation is placed on the outside of a contiguous vapor/air barrier, it is less likely to be interrupted by the primary and secondary structural elements of a building, i.e., the whole frame and the systems' supporting enclosure. |5-8

Heat: Possibility |9-10

The increasing pressures on finite natural resources that come from global demand for construction materials and rising energy consumption are forcing the construction industry to look for

Building Envelopes 70

8 | A window unit at the Faculty of English, consisting of a fixed panel of glazing with fixed shading above and a side-opening ventilation panel protected by weather-shielding louvers. Each window unit sits within an opening in the masonry (block or concrete) wall. The wall was first waterproofed and insulated on the outside, then faced with a terra-cotta rainscreen system.

9 | The Advanced EcoCeramic Envelope System consists of ceramic units made using low-tech, generic, and readily available ram press production methods typically employed in china plate-making.

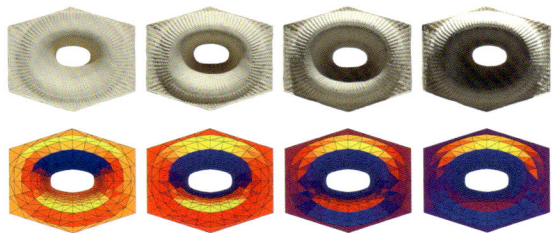

10 | Computer simulations of the EcoCeramic System depict the relative transfer of heat through the modules.

low-impact and less-energy-intensive alternatives. The Advanced EcoCeramic Envelope System seeks to fill the need for a system developed from abundant materials that can meet demanding performance criteria.[2] This envelope system has the capacity to locally mitigate arid climates into habitable thermal ranges through passive cooling techniques.

The EcoCeramics are developed from earthenware clay—a readily available material that can be infinitely reclaimed into high-quality ceramic materials. Clay is produced by the natural forces of erosion on feldspar minerals, which make up the majority of the Earth's crust. The mineral compositions of EcoCeramic are modified for strength and porosity with natural additives and fibers to meet design criteria depending on application, and optimized through thermodynamic modeling and innovative design-development tools in order to employ pattern, texture, coating, and color to manifest different thermal performance results and architectural experiences. Surface strategies from CAD/CAM procedures precisely form the EcoCeramic to provide self-shading and to disrupt airflow over a surface, minimizing heat exchange with the thermal environment and allowing for internal temperatures to maintain greater stability.

In the Advanced EcoCeramic Envelope System, low-tech ceramic manufacturing technologies are combined with computer-generated geometric modules that are specifically calibrated to interact with varying daily and seasonal movements of the sun and are aggregated into complex surface patterns.

Water:
Systems and Collection

Water: Problems |1

Global warming, changing weather patterns, irresponsible planning, increased suburban development, inefficient systems, and waste all contribute to a water supply crisis that is faced globally. Available groundwater is limited and surface-water sources cannot support increased development and demands. Additionally, treated water is often used in circumstances where it is not required—according to an EPA handbook, "While potable water is used almost exclusively for domestic uses, almost 80 percent of demand does not require drinkable water."[1] Water is a valuable commodity, yet it is frequently wasted on runoff from the large, nonporous surfaces that form much of our built environment. Typically,

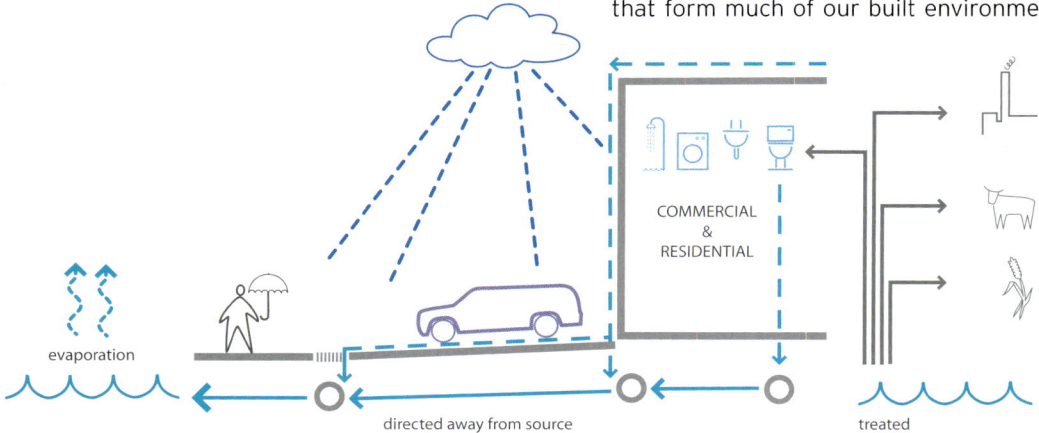

1| Water: problems
The potential of rainwater collection or local management is frequently lost by allowing water runoff from large areas of nonporous building surfaces, including building envelopes.

this potential water resource is directed away on a linear path—it is piped and discharged into streams, rivers, lakes, and oceans rather than recycled to replenish local water sources. The direction, retention, and detention of water are commonly mismanaged causing strain on insufficient or nonexistent municipal systems.

The vast majority of building construction problems are related to water in some way. At the scale of building envelope assemblies, water can erode, rot, and cause mold. The practice of "face-sealing" water out of building envelopes (where a waterproof barrier forms an envelope's outer layer to block any

Building Envelopes   72

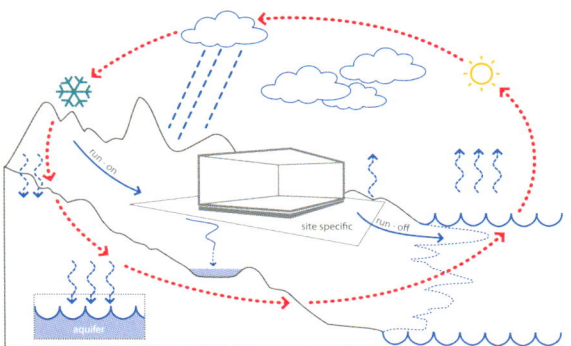

2 | Water: principles (macro scale)
This hydrologic cycle looks at the big picture of water flow through all three physical states: vapor, water, and ice/snow. The whole system operates as a continuous loop, transforming through these three states, and a specific site is always part of this much larger system.

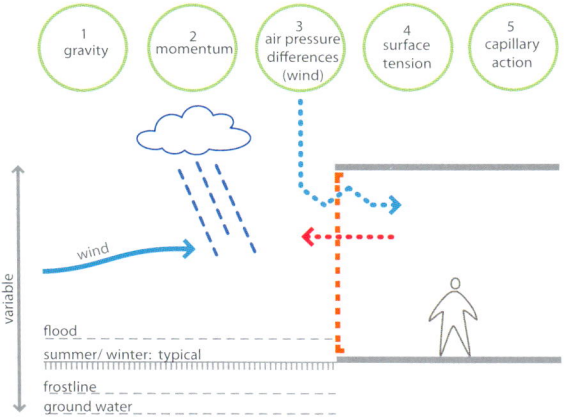

3 | Water: principles (micro scale)
Building envelope strategies are part of a whole surface condition from roof to landscape (hard and soft) and beyond. Building envelopes must address a range of principles related to water. The horizontal condition (specifically roof and ground) has a number of variables to be considered specific to site: climate, prevailing winds, frost, flood, and water-table levels. The vertical condition (specifically wall/window assembly and systems) will be affected by the five ways in which water moves: gravity, momentum, air pressure difference, surface tension, and capillary action.

water ingress) means that they are dependent on the design and quality of their construction details and assemblies to exclude water. If these fail (and they frequently do), water will cause damage—in the form of rain, water vapor, or condensation. Water needs to be addressed at the larger scales of site and infrastructure, as well as at the scale of the detail.

Water: Principles | 2-3

Precipitation and runoff (of rain and surface water) are always site-specific and are part of a larger hydrologic picture, to be taken into account in any design strategy both above and below the ground. Important design considerations include altitude, climate, rainfall, prevailing winds, seasonal changes, groundwater levels, and geology. Information on these factors is available digitally, through sources such as Geographic Information Systems (GIS) and the United States Geological Survey (USGS).

Even water that is perceived as "pure" always contains dissolved minerals and gases as a result of its interaction with the atmosphere, the ground, organic matter, and living organisms. It affects the surfaces and materials it comes into contact with, and it is also affected by them.[2] A more extreme example of this is acid rain, whose high sulfur dioxide content has a corrosive effect on limestone, sandstone, and marble.

Depending on temperature, water changes between three states—solid, liquid, and gas—via transitions known as freezing, thawing, evaporation, condensation, and sublimation. Water moves by means of five different forces—gravity, momentum, air pressure difference, surface tension, and capillary action—all of which will enable penetration into a building envelope assembly. In order to prevent this infiltration, all of these forces must be considered in the design of a building's envelope.[3]

Resistance to water penetration is dependent on the detailing and construction of an assembly,

Elements of a Holistic Approach   73

particularly where interfaces are required between different systems, such as a perimeter flashing and a cladding panel. In principle the path of water must be acknowledged and allowed in some form—through a drain, a pressure-equalization zone, a contiguous barrier, or a weather strip—and constructed and maintained accordingly over the life of a building.

Building envelopes are principally designed to address water in one of three ways: a face-sealed system, which stops all water before it gets through as a first line of defense; a water-managed system, which allows some water through the first line of defense and then directs and drains it out of the system (for example, with a cavity wall construction); or a pressure-equalized system (i.e., a rain screen system), where the pressure differential between the first layer and the second layer of an envelope

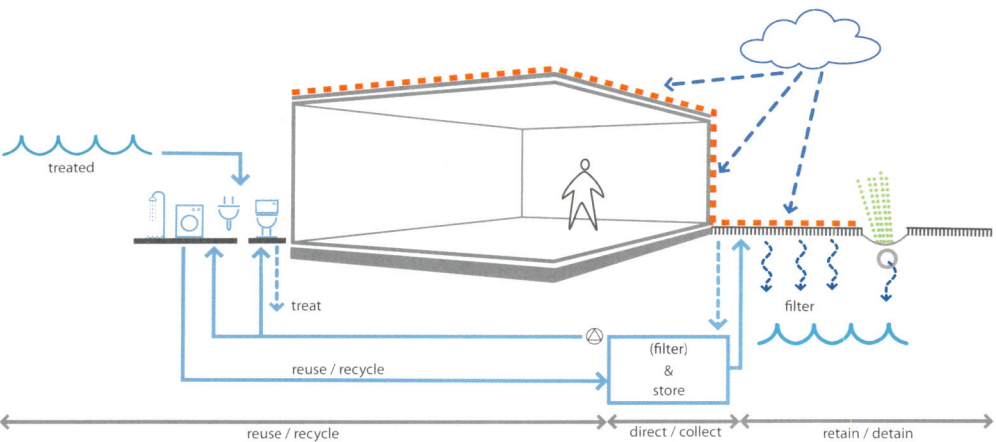

4 | Water: potential
A building envelope must be considered as part of a continuous and varying surface condition (indicated with an orange dashed line in the diagram), able to redirect or collect water for reuse/recycling. In this diagram, the building envelope is placed within the context of a broader water system strategy. Surface water can be filtered and stored locally (shown here in a belowground storage tank) to serve the needs of interior facilities. Recycled wastewater can be used rather than potable water for some interior needs, such as toilet water, as well as to irrigate plantings. Planted swales, shown in green in the diagram, enable filtering and retention of rainwater, allowing it to be managed locally and providing habitat as an alternative to hardscape drainage.

are finely tuned to prevent water from being driven further into the building.

Water penetration must be considered from inside-out as well as outside-in. Airborne water (in vapor or liquid form) from indoor activities such as breathing, washing, and cooking will condense within a wall if it is allowed to enter but not permitted to escape, causing erosion, rot, or mold. If vapor and air barriers are combined in an assembly (see, for example, figures 6 and 7 on p. 70), it is easier to build contiguous protection.

Building Envelopes 74

Water: Potential | 4

The integration of infrastructure systems, landscape, and buildings is essential in order to control, conserve, and reclaim water. By managing water locally at the scale of the site, pollution and runoff can be mitigated and groundwater can be recharged. This could also provide an amenity for building users and a habitat for flora and fauna.

Building envelopes constitute a whole-building surface condition, from roof to landscape (hard and soft) and beyond. Depending on the specific context and location of a project, its water-strategy approach will have different requirements. In an arid climate such as Arizona, where water is scarce, collection and reuse will be priorities, whereas in a wet climate such as Kuala Lumpur, management of humidity and water flow take precedence.

Water can be engaged in a positive way to suit site conditions and climatic opportunities. A body of water adjacent to a building can act as a thermal storage device to impact the microclimate around the building, store energy interseasonally, or act as part of a site's water-management system, as might be found in a reed bed or conditioning lake. Water evaporating into warm, moving air will cause a cooling effect before the air enters a building and improve interior comfort levels by reducing the resultant temperature.

An inch of rainfall can produce six hundred gallons of runoff per one thousand square feet of roof.[4] There is a huge potential for horizontal and vertical building surfaces to be porous and act as on-site filters and collectors of water (e.g., green or brown roofs) rather than relying on piped drainage systems. For a building's vertical surfaces, the percentage of catchment potential (area that can capture water runoff) is lower, depending on envelope profile, rainfall, and prevailing winds, but they should still be part of an overall catchment calculation. The harvesting of rainwater from built surfaces in order to reduce storm runoff and allow reuse on site requires a relatively low capital cost. These harvesting systems identify a catchment area, a means of conveyance from this area (driven by gravity), a storage system (optional), a water treatment system (also optional), and a means of conveyance to the local end use (gravity or pump).[5] Although less rainwater falls on the vertical surfaces of a building, all of the above require direct coordination with—and can be enhanced by—the building envelope's design, so that water is addressed at the scale of the immediate site.

Sustainable drainage systems (SUDS), an alternative approach to piped drainage systems, imitate natural drainage processes with characteristics of storage, slow conveyance, and volume reduction.[6] Every consideration for SUDS is site-specific, and is dependent on soil type, location in the watershed, and local legislation. SUDS aim to reduce both the rate and the volume of water runoff from a building, as well as treat water to remove pollutants as close to the source as possible. A number of techniques can be implemented as SUDS strategies, such as green roofs, porous paving, and retention ponds.

Water: Possibility |5
The Solar Building Envelope System for Water Recycling, Purification, and Thermal Control is a building-integrated solar-absorption strategy for a hybrid, interconnected system of on-site water recovery and occupant comfort control in hot, arid climates.[7] The modulated facade system plugs into a building's infrastructure to allow solar-thermal water pasteurization treatment, providing hot water for distribution to multiple gray-water applications in the building, significantly offsetting demands for water supplies and thermal energy requirements.

The passive, nontracking (i.e., fixed) system is a component assembly, composed of volumetric

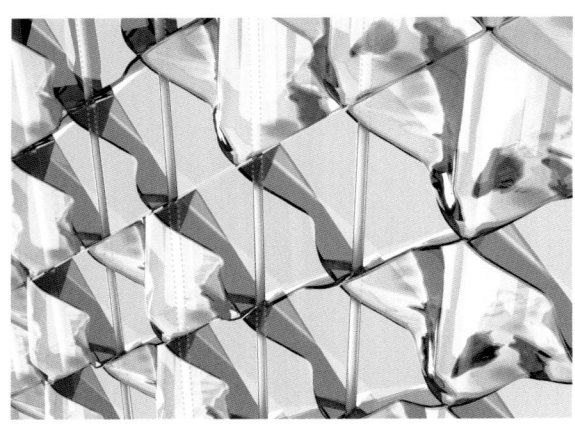

5| The Solar Building Envelope System for Water Recycling, Purification, and Thermal Control purifies water in hot and arid climates.

blocks of transparent glass for maximum solar absorption that are geometrically optimized to concentrate incident solar energy onto water moving through the blocks. Tubes within the blocks circulate treated gray water and actively transfer thermal energy before directing the water to heat exchangers for potable hot water and applications for gray water within the building.

By recovering water on-site, the Solar Building Envelope for Water Recycling, Purification, and Thermal Control will significantly offset building-resource requirements for water and thermal energy while simultaneously providing a building facade system.

**Materials:
Assemblies and Installation**

Materials: Problems
Architects often consider materials as a pick'n'mix application to "compositional and visual surfaces" with little or no bearing on context, performance, life span, or environmental impact.[1] Materials samples—which often are just like paint chips—are sent to architects from manufacturing representatives, added to a firm's materials library, and can be selected without really understanding the implication of one choice over another in terms of where a material comes from, how it performs, or its impact within an assembly.

On-site tolerances and connections between materials rely primarily on caulking—which is often used to hide poor construction, and is an unreliable seal between building components—to maintain building envelope performance. Interfaces between both materials and trades can fall between the gaps (literally) if not considered early in the design process with shared responsibility between designers and contractors. A failure to maintain materials and fabric over the life of the building reduces their value and return on investment.

Elements of a Holistic Approach

Developments in digital modeling and fabrication have enabled highly complex envelopes to be built without regard for the resolution of systems, structure, and services. These aspects of the building are left having to follow its form rather than maximizing their integration to optimize performance.

Smart materials are often used in an additive manner rather than as part of an appropriate design application. For example, at a materials scale, coatings can increase the performance of glass in terms of heat transmission, shading coefficient, and daylight factor, while at a systems scale additional building "layers" can be added, as in a double-skin facade—but are they the right material or system application in the first place?

Materials: Principles
Modern building envelopes consist of a series of additive layers supported in some way by a primary structural system. These layers are composed of transparent (often but not always windows) and solid elements together with an air barrier, a vapor barrier, insulation, and internal and external finishes. Some of these elements may be purposefully combined as one layer.

Building envelope systems that are separate from the primary structure of a building are generally called curtain walls, and can be classified by their method of fabrication and installation as either stick systems or unitized (also known as modular) systems. |1 In stick systems, the components of assembly are constructed piece by piece on-site, whereas a unitized system is composed of large units that are assembled and glazed in a factory, shipped to the site, and erected on the building's structure.[2] |2-5

Systems relate to a grid scale that is determined by internal planning needs, performance, cost, and installation. In office design, a five-foot (United States) or fifteen-hundred-millimeter (Europe) grid

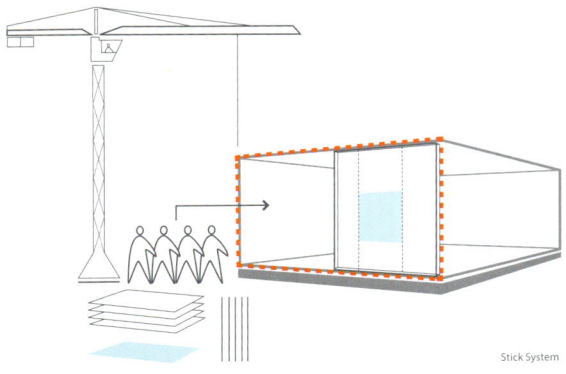

Stick System

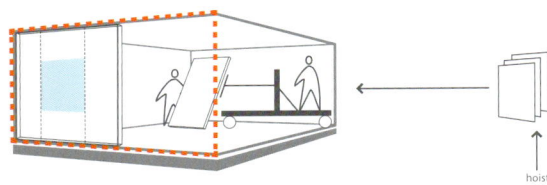

Unitized System

1| Systems installation diagram for stick and unitized systems: A stick system often requires a crane to hoist components into place for installation, as well as a larger on-site construction crew with access equipment to enable them to work safely from the outside of the building. A unitized system can be fabricated in a factory off-site. Dimensioning is dependent on transportation to site and into location (usually with a hoist), but units can be installed from the inside in a shorter amount of time by a smaller crew.

2-5 | A unitized panel is installed on-site for a building in London, England, by architects Allford Hall Monaghan Morris.

is widely used for a number of reasons, primarily ease of handling without relying on a tower crane, size of construction hoist, and flexibility of interior layout, with acoustic separation at the mullions.

Areas of glass in a building are limited by cost, installation, and replacement issues rather than production. A standard glass panel of 10.7 feet by 17 feet (3.3 meters x 5.2 meters) at .25-inch thickness is manufactured in the United States for supply distribution to fabricators, but it has limited performance: it has to be transported, engineered to resist wind load over its area, is harder to install and replace, is less flexible in terms of dividing the space it encloses, and limits potential change of use from, say, commercial to residential.[3]

In the case of the Tooley Street offices by Allford Hall Monaghan Morris (see pp. 106–9), the architects considered the overall performance of the building envelope as part of an integrated approach to structure, skin, and systems. A desire for maximum flexibility within the office space was balanced with cost: what would bring the most value to building users over time versus how much flexibility would be required should the offices ever be replanned. The architects weighed the options with the client and decided that placing windows in areas that would give the building's users the greatest feeling of "openness" would provide the most value. The offices are just as light as one would expect from any modern space, but the envelope has a 50 percent window area rather than 100 percent. With a slight reduction in flexibility (in this case, removing every third mullion against which to fix an internal partition), day-to-day comfort and performance of the building have been greatly enhanced.

While we draw materials in construction documents with single straight lines, in reality things are irregular, and will deviate from the idealized lines. Materials move due to thermal and moisture

Elements of a Holistic Approach   79

6-7| This corner junction of the Institute of Criminology by Allies and Morrison (see pp. 116-23) was three-dimensionally modeled (figure 6) and reviewed with the cladding contractor (Grupa Schneider) to fully coordinate design intent, performance, and buildability during design development. Figure 7 shows the corner junction as built.

expansion and contraction, and deform due to dead loads or applied loads, such as wind suction or pressure. Deviations also result from variations in fabrication and construction processes. A concrete structure, for example, can vary in tolerance by half an inch (depending on where in the world it is being built)—this means it can vary by an inch over a certain dimension, and cumulatively, it could be off even more. A building envelope system has to take these deviations into account for stability, safety, air leakage, fire stops, and watertightness.

Tolerance is not drawn per se in a plan or section; instead it is included in a written specification document that accompanies the set of construction drawings. Digital modeling can account for tolerance, but essentially we still specify tolerances separately in construction documents, whether for a subassembly or a single component. Modeling, testing, and dialogue with both engineers and contractors early in the design process is more likely to identify the areas where tolerances might be tight on-site, allowing for their resolution or minimization through design before construction commences. |6-7

With a greater degree of prefabrication in a controlled factory environment, it is possible to achieve much tighter tolerances within building envelope assemblies. A process of multiple quality checks by material suppliers, subcontractors, and through on-site inspections can often lead to a product that is of a greater quality than industry standards require.[4] |8-9

Materials: Potential

Design of building envelopes (and buildings as a whole) is finally being reconnected with production. The initial construction costs and associated ongoing running costs of a building's enclosure are a huge expenditure that should be considered from every aspect throughout the design, production,

Building Envelopes 80

8 | Bespoke aluminum cladding components await assembly in a factory making unitized cladding panels for Liftschutz Davidson Sandilands' Charlotte Building (see pp. 140–47).

9 | Precast concrete cladding components were fabricated in Belgium and assembled in Poland to make unitized cladding panels for Allies and Morrison's Institute of Criminology (see pp. 116–23).

installation, occupation, and disassembly processes. Digital technologies such as building information modeling (BIM) present tools to enable dialogue between designers, industry (suppliers and fabricators), installers, and facilities management.

Fabricators and contractors who are brought into the design process not only constructively contribute to the discussion of buildability, they also bring with them knowledge of the supply chain. In terms of sustainability, this is a way of reconnecting sourcing of materials to the design team without the traditional contractual obligations of explicit specification.

In his book *Buildability in Practice*, Ian Ferguson states that "Buildability is concerned with...putting together assemblies and sub-assemblies, often in bad weather and at all seasons of the year, when hands are frozen and legs are knee deep in mud," and that regardless of developments in prefabrication, site work will always be part of the reality of building.[5] This is true, but developments in computer-aided design and manufacturing (CAD/CAM) in particular have allowed for much more off-site fabrication and assembly of building envelopes. Automated fabrication has enabled more complicated assemblies and specialized integration for unitized systems to be built in the controlled environment of the factory in more efficient ways.

While ultimately system and material applications for building envelopes must be appropriate to the context of the design, advances in material science for composite materials, coatings, and films are enabling specified materials to work harder to meet performance criteria. Professor Paul J. Donnelly and his team at Washington University in St. Louis are researching a holistic approach to the use of phase change materials (PCMs) as part of building envelope and systems performance.[6] PCMs store and release energy as they change state from a liquid to solid and vice versa. They have been used

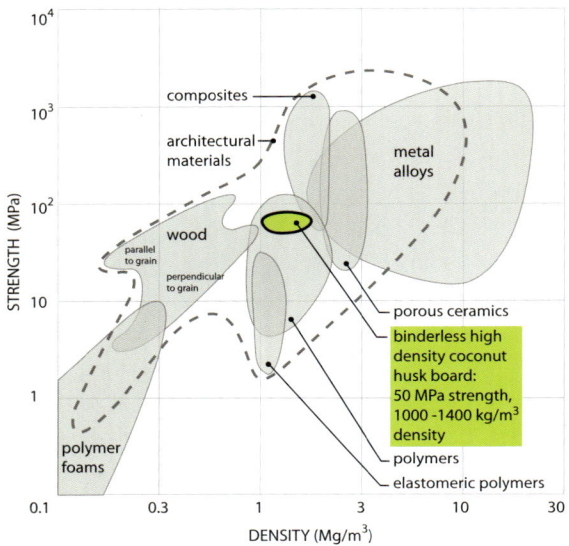

10| When binderless, high-density Coconut Husk Boards are compared to typical values of other material categories, it is found that their strength is comparable to or exceeds that of most architectural wood products.

11| Coconut husks, the raw material for Coconut Husk Boards.

12| Coconut Husk Boards, developed by a team at CASE, are made from post-agricultural waste and can be fabricated at multiple scales and configurations.

in clothing and product design for their thermal comfort properties but have been slow to enter the building market due to affordability and application. By "sucking up" unwanted heat in an internal space, a PCM can play a part in holding on to solar heat gain, delaying release in order to limit discomfort, reduce peak loads on systems, and potentially utilize the thermal energy at a later time when it is needed more. This material application could bridge the gap between aesthetics and comfort by being inserted into the building envelope assembly or internal wall construction.

Materials: Possibility |10-12

A team at Rensselaer Polytechnic Institute's Center for Architecture Science and Ecology (CASE) are investigating the viability of developing structural materials from the post-agricultural waste of coconut husks, which can be milled and manufactured into multiple low-cost building products for use in tropical hot and humid climates.

Coconut Husk Board promises to be a viable and high-performing substitute for imported wood-based products, especially in the tropics, where a substantial volume of husk from coconut production can be reclaimed and processed into building materials at an industrial scale.[7] Intrinsic lignin biopolymers in these husks eliminate the need for synthetic binders in high-performance sheathing boards.

When manufactured as a desiccant board, the coconut husk absorbs water vapor, creating a drier, more comfortable internal environment. The proposed building-prototype designs integrate Coconut Husk Boards with passive cooling strategies to provide greater comfort, with the potential to reduce energy consumption in a broad range of housing types.

Daylighting:
Comfort and Control

Daylighting—the illumination of a space by sunlight—is not purely a matter of quantity and measurement. Decades of research have shown that access to natural light increases our well-being, comfort, and productivity—we are visual-centric beings. A building's envelope provides access to daylight—with fluctuation, direction, color, and shadow—as well as a view and connection to the exterior from our internal environments.[1]

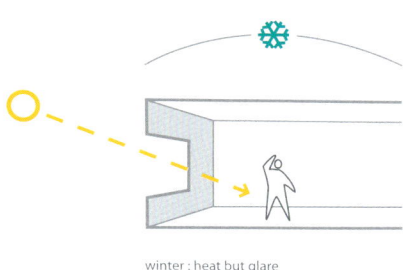
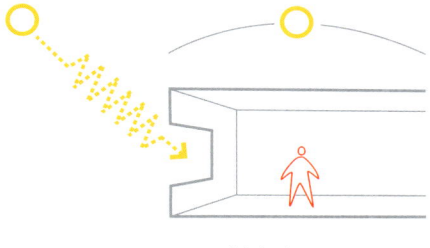

winter : heat but glare

summer : light but heat

1| Daylight: problems

Daylight: Problems |1

A need for deep-plan buildings and maximized square footage, along with developments in artificial lighting systems and the availability of air-conditioning, have led to increased plan-to-envelope ratios. As a result, daylight is no longer utilized at maximum efficiency to illuminate interior spaces. Often, large areas of poorly oriented and unshaded glazing expose building interiors to direct sunlight and affect building-user comfort—blinds are dropped to reduce glare through windows, and artificial lights are switched on to make up for blocked daylight, all at the expense of energy consumption.

The fundamental predicament of daylighting is that when the solar angle is higher (around the summer solstice) the sun is also at its hottest—we want the light, but not the heat gain. When the solar angle is lower (around the winter solstice) we want the light and heat, but not the associated glare from the low-angle sun.

Required light levels are based on the worst-case scenario—a completely overcast day—and relate to overall light levels of a space rather than the perception of the building user, their visual tasks, or context. Light levels are often measured on the basis of reading and writing at a horizontal plane (such as a desk). However, office work and planning now involve the ubiquitous use of personal computers, with flat, vertical screens.

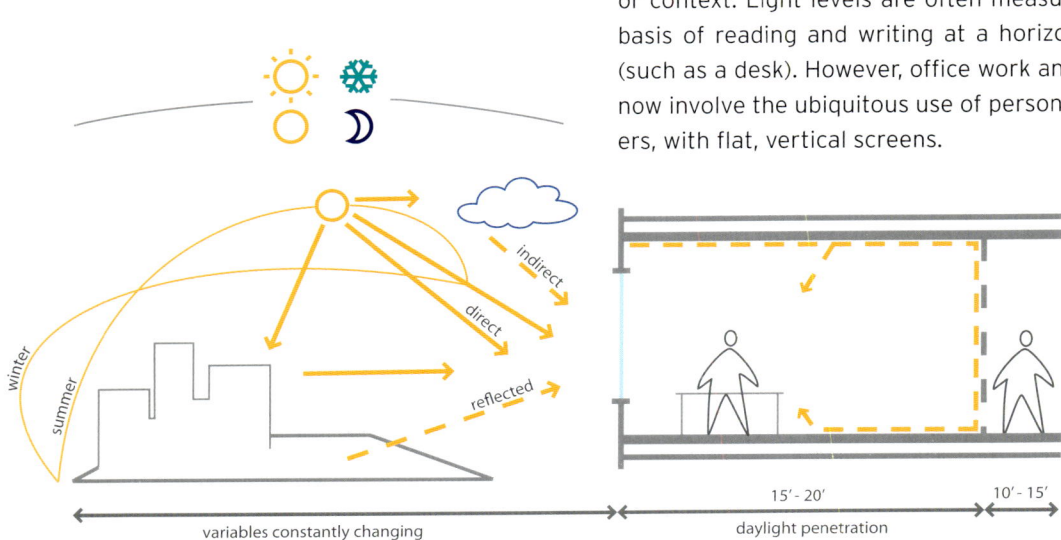

2 | Daylight: principles
This diagram identifies the means by which daylight and direct sunlight penetrate interior space. Since variables are constantly changing, depending on time of day, season, cloud cover, and adjacencies (such as neighboring buildings or planting), daylight factor is used to calculate the effectiveness of daylight to carry out specified tasks. The orientation and ratio of plan depth to width and solar angle are also critical in daylight penetration.

Daylight: Principles |2
The angle and path of the sun are specific to location and circumstance, and they constantly change over time. Daylight and sunlight are transmitted to interiors directly or indirectly (by reflection from adjacent buildings or surfaces through the building envelope). This transmission is affected not only by geographic location but also by any immediate adjacencies (overshadowing buildings, a body of water, vegetation and planting, and so on) or surrounding building surfaces.

Light is usually measured in foot-candles or lux levels, but due to the general inconsistency of daylight levels, "daylight factor" is the unit used when looking at daylight levels. Daylight factor (DF) is a measure of the effectiveness of daylight indoors, and is calculated as a percentage ratio between illumination indoors and outdoors on an average overcast day (with dirty windows). A DF of between 2 and 5 percent is considered "a good balance between lighting and thermal aspects."[2] If a building's DF is

3| Working model for a gallery space of the Brandhorst Museum

Figures 3 and 4: In their design for the Brandhorst Museum in Munich, Germany, architects Sauerbruch Hutton integrated daylight as a key part of the galleries' lighting plan. The transverse gallery shown here (approximately 23 feet high from floor to ceiling) is lit in part by a large window at the side. This provides ideal conditions for sculptures and three-dimensional objects, and also creates a direct visual contact with the street. In the museum's other exhibition spaces, bright daylight (up to 100,000 lux in the summer) is filtered through light blades in front of the windows, reducing it to gallery-appropriate levels (approximately 300 lux). Daylight ceilings of translucent fabric provide uniform distribution of natural light from rooflights and reduce any strong variations in light levels.

4| A naturally lit gallery in the Brandhorst Museum as built

greater than 5 percent, heat gain in the summer and heat loss in the winter through glass area are likely to become problems.

Heat gain and light must be considered together according to the needs of an internal space if comfort is to be achieved for building users. In numeric terms, these are measured by the solar heat gain coefficient (SHGC) and visible light transmittance (VLT), respectively. SHGC indicates how well an area of glass blocks heat from sunlight—measured between zero and one. The higher the value, the more heat is transmitted through the glass.[3] VLT is the percentage of total visible light that passes through a glazing system. Low-transmission glazing makes interiors darker, and our "time orientation is…fed distorted and unexpected data"—in other words, it affects our comfort levels.[4]

In some cases heat gain may be welcomed, depending on where you are in the world. In cooler climates the thermal performance of glass (measured as a U-value) in a window or wall becomes more critical, since the ratio of daylight to thermal loss from a building is especially important. Seasonal cycles and location have to be considered as well—many temperate, continental climates have both cold winters and hot (possibly humid) summers.

More daylight is not necessarily better—reflections and contrast have a significant effect on the visual comfort of a room. If changes in light levels between spaces are too extreme, our eyes do not have sufficient time to adjust, and our perception of lightness or darkness is altered. For example, if we move from a brightly lit circulation space into a naturally lit room with lower light levels, we might consider the naturally lit space to be too dark, even though its light levels are actually appropriate to the tasks and needs for that space. At the scale of a surface, if there is a stark light-level contrast between a window and a surrounding wall, discomfort can occur from the glare of the window.

Elements of a Holistic Approach   85

The light levels at all thresholds, internal and external, need to be considered in terms of their sequence of occupation, adjacency, and use. |3-4

Daylight penetration isn't the only concern when designing a window or area of glazing—views, a connection to the outside, and access also play a role in the quality and perception of a space. Sunlight can be pleasant as long as it does not cause discomfort. A person in a west-facing office might feel discomfort due to glare and heat gain from direct, mid-afternoon sunlight—whereas the same effect in a residential unit might be quite pleasant. Design

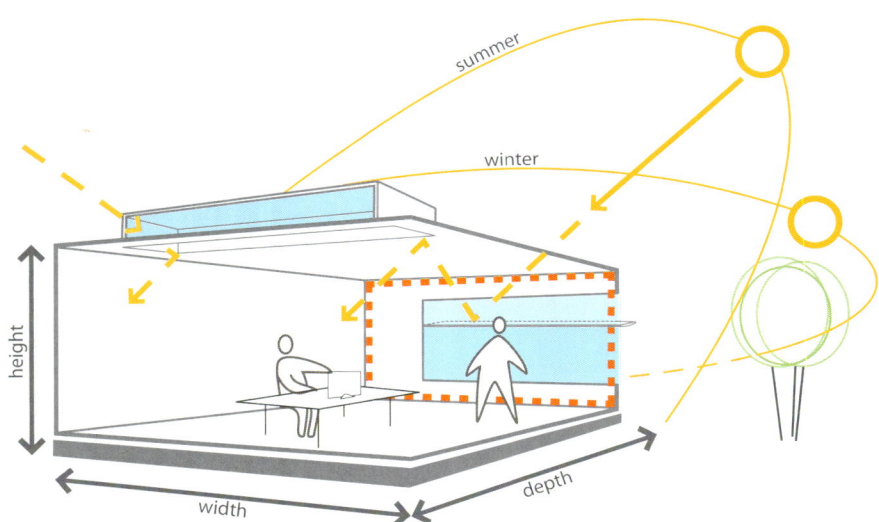

5| Daylight: potential
The integrated design of a building's envelope, services, and form is essential for good daylight provision. The coordination of diffuse daylight strategies during a building's early design stages (through the use of light shelves or screens, for example) and a comprehensive understanding of the potential light (direct, indirect, and reflected) of a site play a part in effective design.

considerations must start with understanding the activity of a building's users—what will the primary function of an interior space be, and how might this change over time?

Daylight: Potential |5

Good, well-balanced daylighting through a building's envelope will increase user comfort levels and reduce artificial light levels, peak loads, and energy consumption. This is does not, however, require a completely glazed building envelope—25 to 30 percent of wall area (10 to 20 percent floor area)

Building Envelopes   86

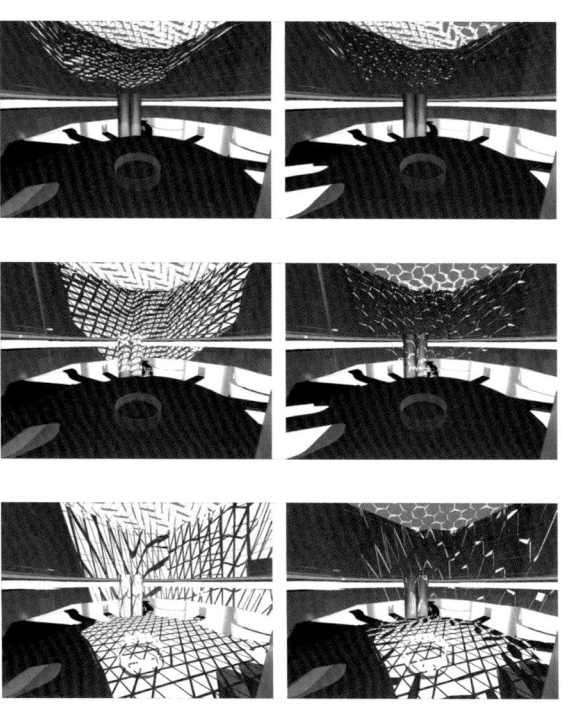

6| Solar-shading studies were modeled to test the Hoberman system's effects prior to construction. The three studies in the left column show lighting conditions throughout the day when the shades are fully retracted. The studies in the right column show the shades partially deployed for the following times, from top to bottom: 8 AM in March, 10 AM in April, and noon in June.

7| A module of the Hoberman-designed linear shading system, with shading fully opened on the left and fully retracted on the right

is sufficient for most commercial and residential buildings to achieve good daylight levels.[5] As a rule of thumb, daylight will penetrate up to between fifteen and twenty feet into a building, and will give sufficient light for secondary tasks for an additional ten to fifteen feet beyond that. Light shelves, scoops, and reflectors can assist in maximizing the potential of available light, projecting daylight more evenly and further into a plan's depth. For example, a correctly engineered light shelf can assist in shading heat gain from a lower portion of glazing while reflecting light back into a building through an upper portion of glazing—providing a more diffuse "up-lighting" directed across the ceiling.

Shading should always be integrated on a commercial building's south- and west-facing facades—and sometimes on the north-facing facade, depending on geographic location—to avoid discomfort from glare and unwanted heat gain (in the northern hemisphere). Shading is most effective when located outside of an envelope's glass, on the principle that heat gain has less impact if you can stop it from coming into the building as much as possible.

Artificial light is a major component of energy consumption. The control and coordination of daylight penetration with artificial lighting in terms of type, layout, switching operation, and overrides through a building management system (BMS) must be integrated with a building envelope strategy.

Daylight: Possibility |6-8

Designer Chuck Hoberman's work with Hoberman Associates is based on action, performance, activity, and transformation. The folding-surface structures the firm designs consist of many connected pieces that enable continuous, three-dimensional transformations. Structural integrity is maintained through key geometric features, which are held invariant even as they transform between radically different sizes or shapes. Hoberman Associates'

8 | As seen in this rendering of the Audiencia Provincial, the Hoberman shading system prevents direct sunlight from penetrating the interior glass walls of the offices while allowing the maximum amount of light into the central atrium.

work is about relationships, and it emerges out of context and requirements.[6]

The firm collaborated with Foster + Partners on a new appeals court in Madrid (the Audiencia Provincial), creating a dynamic surface structure that minimizes unwanted solar gain while allowing natural daylight inside the building. As a key part of the building's environmental strategy, Hoberman was contracted to develop several customized shading systems. These shading units will occupy the court's circular central atrium and eight peripheral atria, and they are inspired by the dappled light that shines through the leaves of a tree. The shades are hexagonal in shape and conform to the diagrid structure of the roof. They are composed of a series of perforated metal slats, attached to pivoting arms that allow the slats to move laterally and retract into a slender bundle that visually aligns with the roof's structure.

An algorithm combining historic solar-gain data with real-time light-level sensing will control the shading units. Transformation will be integrated with a BMS so it can be coordinated with a number of elements in the building, such as artificial lighting control and cooling systems.

Fabricated from aluminum and steel, each unit is driven by a servomotor with custom-array control. When activated, the units extend to form a continuous surface composed of a series of slats that can be made of different materials, including metal, plastic, and wood. This linear system can be designed in nonrectangular shapes and installed in a non-vertical orientation, responding in smooth and controlled movements to the constant changes of daylight specific to site and season.

Building Envelopes

Energy:
Minimizing and Maximizing

> Reducing potable water demand by 10 percent could save approximately 300 billion kilowatt hours of energy each year in the U.S.... Reduced water demand provided by rainwater harvesting systems translates directly to energy savings.
>
> —Christopher Kloss

Energy: Problems

Our consumption of fossil fuels has accelerated global warming through carbon dioxide emissions. Nearly half (48 percent) of all annual energy consumption and carbon emissions in the United States are associated with energy use in buildings, and 76 percent of all power-plant-generated electricity is used just to operate buildings: heating, cooling, lighting, hot water, and the plug load (electrical use from equipment powered by plugging into an outlet).[1] Most of these uses are directly affected by a perimeter enclosure condition in a building.

Data regarding energy use and carbon emissions is widely circulated, but it is often examined out of context and without consideration for the way people actually occupy and utilize space. A low-rise office building will likely consume less energy per square foot than an inner city high-rise but consume greater energy per capita. Architect and energy expert Michelle Addington explains this, writing, "High-rise buildings generally have more than twice the number of occupants per square foot as low-rise buildings," and "the typical high-rise building uses 50 to 70 percent less energy per person than does the typical low-rise building."[2] Energy efficiency is expressed in $kWh/m^2/yr$, which relates to physical space but not to inhabitation. Energy data statistics, energy use comparisons between building types, and the ways occupants think about the energy they are responsible for using are often difficult to correlate.

A widespread desire for glass commercial buildings with window areas far greater than the percentage required to achieve comfortable light levels—and with high conductivity—is directly at odds with the need to curb heating- and cooling-related energy use. Equally, buildings that do not take advantage of daylighting through appropriate building envelope design waste energy on artificial lighting.

Embodied energy and life-cycle metrics often consider only individual materials or components rather than whole assemblies and systems, such as a building envelope and its performance over time.

Energy: Principles
The performance of a building's envelope is pivotal to the energy consumption of both commercial and residential projects, albeit in different ways. Housing typically has a greater envelope-to-volume ratio, meaning that energy consumption is greater for heating and cooling and less for lighting and plug loads.[3] On the other hand, commercial buildings usually have a greater volume-to-envelope ratio, necessitating higher energy use for lighting than in housing. Additionally, plug loads for commercial buildings are dramatically higher than in residential buildings due to greater occupancy.[4]

The energy related to a building must be considered from two different perspectives: the embodied energy of the materials from which it is constructed, including the recurring embodied energy of materials required for maintenance, repair, and replacement during its life; and the energy required to run the building, along with the carbon emissions related to that energy use.[5] The former relates to building fabric, the latter to building occupation.

In a typical office building, approximately 26 percent of its total embodied energy (the acquisition, processing, manufacturing, transportation, and construction of raw materials) is associated with its envelope. The longer a building lasts, the greater its recurring embodied energy. However, the operating energy of a typical office represents 85 percent of total-building energy at the end of a 50-year life span—as a building gets older, its operating needs go up, since the building fabric deteriorates to an extent over time.[6]

The reduction of a building's energy consumption should be addressed in the following order with regard to capital and operational costs: increasing systems efficiency and reducing loads; introducing passive systems such as massing, material specification, and solar utilization; and lastly, applying active systems such as photovoltaic panels. This order is based on a return on investment, the first reduction being the simplest and least expensive to implement if addressed early on in the design process.

Metering mechanisms are used to assess carbon dioxide emissions and energy efficiency, and energy consumption can also be compared to benchmarks. Through metering and post-occupancy evaluation we can understand what, when, and how occupants use energy. For example, the largest single energy use in buildings is electricity.[7] Electricity meter data generally registers as a lump-sum figure, with no way to differentiate between use for lighting versus cooling versus plug loads (such as computers, lamps, fans, and space heaters). Submeters can break down "building" loads (the energy needed to run the building's systems) from "process" loads (such as plug-in computers) and allow identification of increased peak loads and energy usage over time, throughout the day and year, so designers and building users can specifically assess how energy is used.

Best-practice reference standards such as LEED (Leadership in Energy and Environmental Design, in the United States) and BREEAM (Building Research Establishment Environmental Assessment Method, in the United Kingdom) are two examples of environmental measurements for the performance of a building. LEED gives points for the design of building envelopes and systems that maximize energy performance as part of a whole building rating. It calls

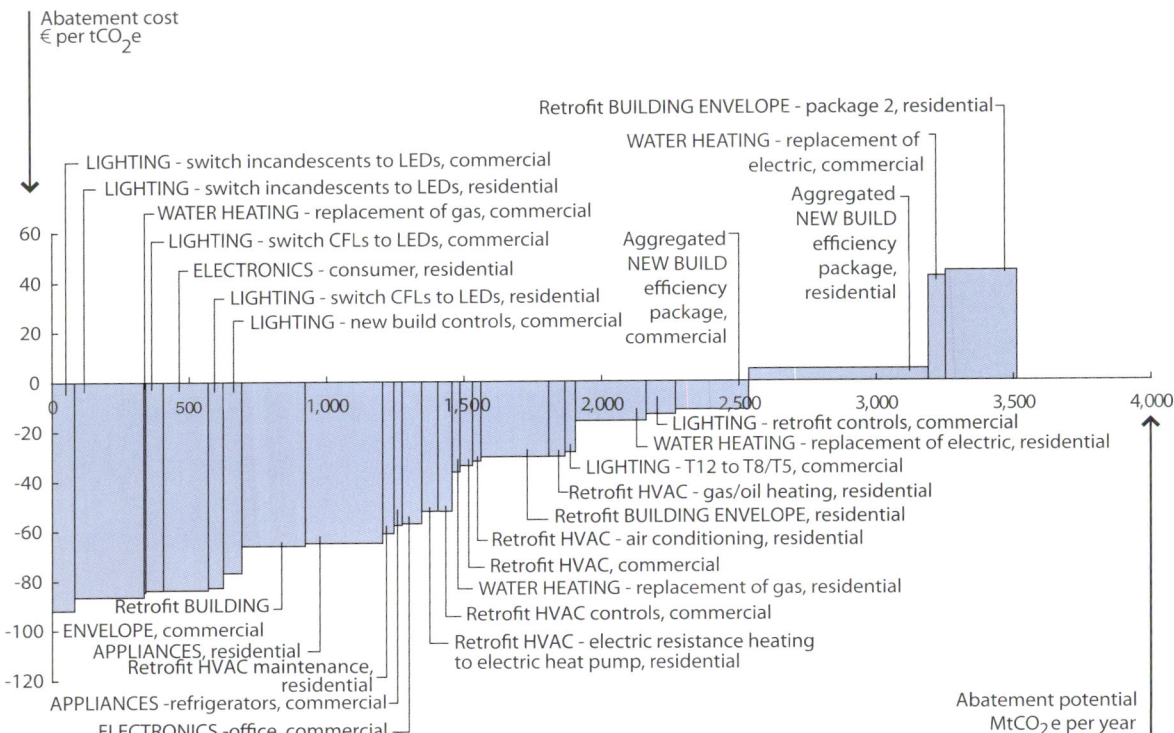

1| This greenhouse-gas abatement cost-curve diagram by McKinsey & Company provides a quantitative basis for discussions about what actions would be most effective in reducing emissions and how much they might cost. This extract shows abatement measures specifically related to the building sector—primary areas of address are directly related to the building envelope: insulation, airtightness, passive-solar utilization, and lighting. The y axis measures abatement cost in Euros per metric tons of carbon dioxide emissions (the cost to make the reduction in emissions), and the x axis shows the abatement energy-savings potential (reduction in emissions potential), in million metric tons of carbon dioxide per year. The thicker bars indicate greater emissions abatement potential for less cost.

for the use of a computer simulation model to assess performance and to identify the most cost-effective energy measures. Energy performance must be compared to that of a baseline building, as established by the American Society of Heating, Refrigerating and Air-Conditioning Engineers (ASHRAE) Standard 90.1. A baseline building meets the requirements of building code and legislation as it stands and is relative to current ASHRAE standards.

Energy: Possibility

Since buildings are responsible for such a large proportion of energy consumption, they are potentially a huge part of the solution—any change in the building sector will have a global effect. Dramatic reductions in energy consumption and carbon emissions are possible with the application of fundamental, but not complicated, changes. Research into greenhouse gas (GHG) abatement by consultants McKinsey & Company shows that there is potential to reduce GHG emissions in 2030 by 35 percent compared with 1990 levels. This reduction could be even greater if inhabitant behavior can be changed, i.e., if users start to take more responsibility for their interaction with the environment. |1 Figure 1 shows the portion of the study related directly to the building sector.

There are four major categories of abatement opportunities: energy efficiency, low-carbon energy supply, terrestrial carbon, and behavioral changes. In terms of building envelope performance, energy efficiency is directly related to airtightness and insulation performance. Effective design and maximum efficiency can be achieved without compromising design criteria.

To address energy efficiency in a building, its localized and regional site—including site shading, vegetation, orientation, and prevailing winds—must be considered first and foremost. Passive cooling and natural ventilation, when combined with appropriate window ratios and sunshading strategies, can reduce mechanical systems demand significantly in both residential and commercial buildings. Professor Joel Loveland, director of the University of Washington's BetterBricks Integrated Design Lab and an expert in daylighting design, states that "Buildings that take advantage of diffuse, well-shaded daylight for illumination of critical task spaces can often reduce their electrical use by more than 40 percent through the reduction of electric lighting requirements and peak cooling demand."[8] It is easy to understand the huge potential daylighting has for the reduction of carbon emissions and pollutants when considering that lighting accounts for about 20-25 percent of the total energy consumption and even 30-40 percent in the commercial sector.[9] Business hours coincide with daylight hours, and naturally lit buildings reduce electricity

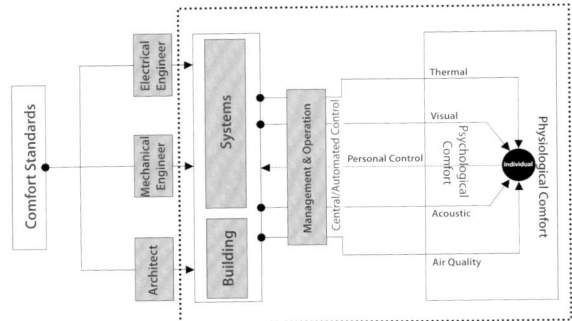

2| This diagram shows the conventional approach to providing comfort in building design practice, where emphasis is on mechanical and electrical systems and where consultants operate independently from each other.

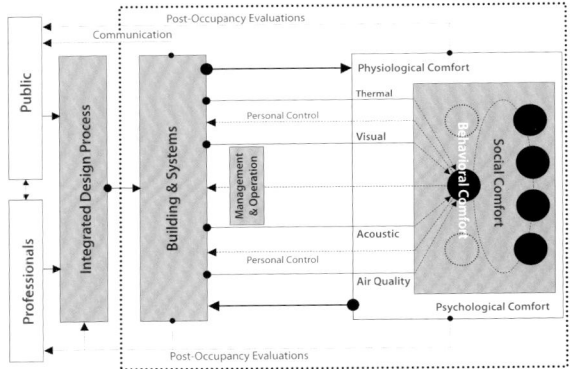

3| This diagram explains an emerging expansion of the notion of comfort: a building and inhabitant system that aims for interactivity, with flexibility to adapt to the changing needs of the entire system over an extended time.

loads and allow the building users to play a role in the control of lighting, contributing significantly to user satisfaction.

Behavior changes related to building enclosure require a paradigm shift from steady-state expectations—where building performance is largely invisible to users—to a raised awareness of users, operators, and managers. Inhabitants must be "active, committed, and knowledgeable," interacting directly with a building's envelope and systems to have some degree of control over daily comfort.[10] To quote Kathryn Janda of the Environmental Change Institute at Oxford University, "Buildings don't use energy: people do," and in the face of climate change designers need to prepare inhabitants for an interactive role and seek ways of integrating user involvement.[11] A building's envelope provides its most tangible opportunity of interaction and control, at a threshold between external and internal environments. |2-3

Energy: Potential |4-5

The Integrated Concentrating (IC) system is a building-integrated photovoltaic solar facade system that substantially reduces the cost of solar energy.[12] The system has a dramatically different approach from existing flat-plate or concentrating photovoltaic (PV) technologies, and it presents an integrated strategy for solar generated electrical power supply, thermal energy, enhanced day-lighting, and reduced solar gain through the incorporation of translucent concentrating modules into double-skin curtain wall systems.

The IC system is composed of multiple glass modules that track the sun and concentrate solar rays with a Fresnel lens surface. These concentrating modules are situated within a glass facade or atrium roof of a building and mounted on a highly accurate, inexpensive tracking mechanism that is able to follow the path of the sun. The system

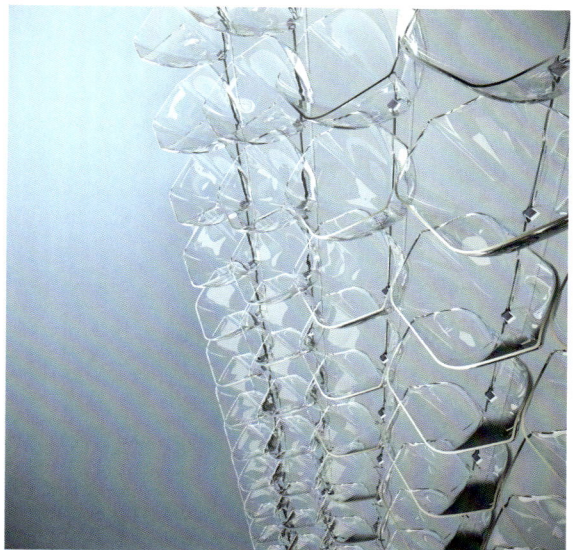

4 | The Integrated Concentrating (IC) solar facade system—designed by Anna Dyson (CASE/RPI), Michael Jensen, a mechanical engineer at RPI, and Peter Stark, a Harvard physicist—maximizes the capturing and utilization of solar energy through a building envelope.

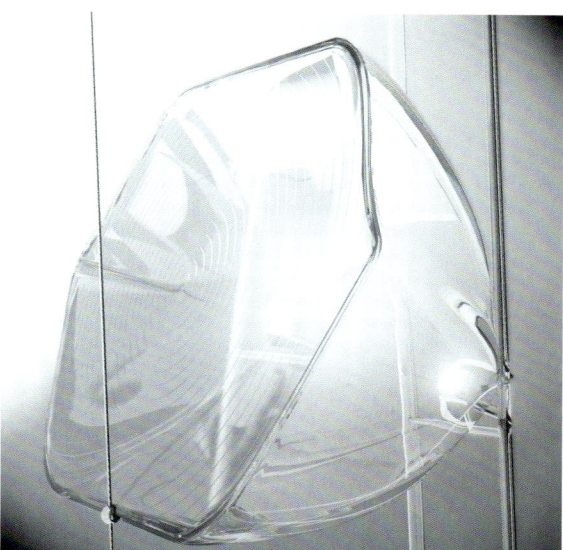

5 | The facade's modules are made of borosilicate glass and attach to a glass tubular structural system.

capitalizes on the structural components, encasements, and maintenance schedules of existing facade systems and uses minimal and inexpensive materials.

PV panels currently operate at a 15 to 20 percent efficiency rate. The IC system is far more efficient, though, because it tracks the path of the sun to maximize energy transfer and uses concentrating solar cells, which currently have a 35 percent operating efficiency rate, for electrical production. Through further research, these solar cells are projected to have the potential of more than 50 percent efficiency in the future. Additionally, approximately 40 percent of the remaining waste heat is recovered from the building facade and converted into high quality heat (a higher temperature form of heat that can be transferred further distances with greater efficiency), which can power cooling systems. In this way, the IC system inverts conventional models of dealing with heat and light that shine on buildings because it does not reject the direct solar gain to the building, but rather it transforms the qualities of the incoming energy and redirects the flow so the energy can be fully harnessed and utilized. Instead of using opaque shading surfaces, transparent modules actively concentrate, use, and remove solar energy before it is transferred through the building envelope as heat, converting a low-quality, diffuse energy source into a higher quality form that can be used to drive building systems such as cooling.

The architectural integration of the IC system ensures an efficient transfer of electric and thermal energy into interior applications while reducing solar gain and enhancing daylight penetration. It also allows for the possibility of shading or daylighting a space through transparent surfaces by redirecting direct solar beams while allowing diffuse light to flood interior spaces. Energy production projections for the IC system show cost payback periods that are substantially below those of existing solar-energy systems.

Section III: Integrated Building Envelope Strategies

The ultimate task of architecture is to act in favor of human beings—to interpose itself between people and the natural environment.

–James Marston Fitch, *American Building: The Forces That Shape It*

The case studies in this section identify specific examples that have successfully negotiated the complexities that come with "live" projects. They exemplify how a strong design idea is essential to navigate and bind layered and multiple issues—and show that understanding the "why" as much as the "how" of assemblage is critical to the work of the building design team. There are many ways to solve a problem; the trick is to understand why you might choose one solution over another.

The following buildings address specific design challenges posed by a range of contextual requirements: developing a housing envelope versus an office envelope, integrating passive environmental strategies, understanding users' requirements and their notions of comfort, enabling adaptability, and realizing value through design. Here, these challenges have been capitalized on through integrated design to make successful architecture.

Live/Work

Adelaide Wharf Housing and 160 Tooley Street Offices, London, England
Allford Hall Monaghan Morris

> Buildings are continuously overglazed because people can easily measure the percentage of glazing—when what actually matters is the perception of glazing from inside and outside and the quality of light.
> —Simon Allford

Architecture practice Allford Hall Monaghan Morris's (AHMM) approach to the design of a building envelope, regardless of program type, is to first clearly understand the constraints of the project: program, site, context, planning, legislation, and economics. These parameters then become design drivers, maximizing possibility rather than constraining it. This approach has produced integrated solutions in response to complex issues for a variety of program types. Adelaide Wharf and 160 Tooley Street are examples of housing and office projects that AHMM have recently completed in London. |1-2

Housing and offices have very different spatial needs, but some of the most flexible, and perhaps best enjoyed, spaces for both have been adapted from the warehouse loft model, where the building has a robust shell housing flexible internal space, large windows and light wells or internal courts give access to daylight and air, and high ceilings give a generous sense of space. The two projects shown here are in part derived from this building type and context, combined with the benefits of unitized, prefabricated cladding construction. |3-4

AHMM developed Adelaide Wharf from a general study of housing for low-income workers in London. It is a pioneering, mixed-tenure housing scheme comprising 147 new homes and 7,000 square feet of office space in a C-shaped, six-story courtyard building. |5 The envelope, form, and planning of the building were carefully considered as a unified whole, in which privately owned apartments, shared-ownership units, and social housing are indistinguishable from each other.

1| 160 Tooley Street: Looking down Shand Street, with facade of 160 Tooley Street visible

opposite:
2| Adelaide Wharf: Suspended balconies, looking north down Queensbridge Road

Partly renovation and partly new construction, 160 Tooley Street is a mixed-use development of flexible office space, retail space, and residential units. |6 The client and architect adopted innovative approaches for all aspects of the building's design, procurement, and construction. Tooley Street's contractor partnered with AHMM in the design process six months before construction started on-site, allowing a high degree of coordination both between disciplines and with key subcontractors/fabricators. This arrangement fully exploited the benefits of prefabrication for highly finished elements, such as exposed structure and facade materials, and enabled the creation of a holistic, integrated design.

3| A precedent photograph of the existing site at 160 Tooley Street from AHMM's library

Designing Envelopes for Housing: Adelaide Wharf

The residential plans at Adelaide Wharf are cellular in nature, and the varying room widths within them drive the facade bay sizes. This sets up a repeatable module that accommodates these room widths. By planning the units so that all service spaces (bathrooms, kitchens, and circulation) are in the interior of the plan, the facade is left to be entirely populated by habitable rooms that require windows. |7

4| Interior of Britannia Street, a previous warehouse-based conversion project carried out by AHMM

The two room types that have window walls are bedrooms and living rooms. These spaces have different appropriate window sizes, types, and positions. Large-paned windows suit the deep-plan living rooms, giving good daylight and sunlight penetration, as well as views out. Smaller windows give bedrooms more privacy and solid wall area to suit their furniture layouts within efficient room areas. Since the bedroom windows are smaller, they can be offset in different positions, and arranged to stagger rather than stack, as the living room windows do. This sets up a repetition of two window

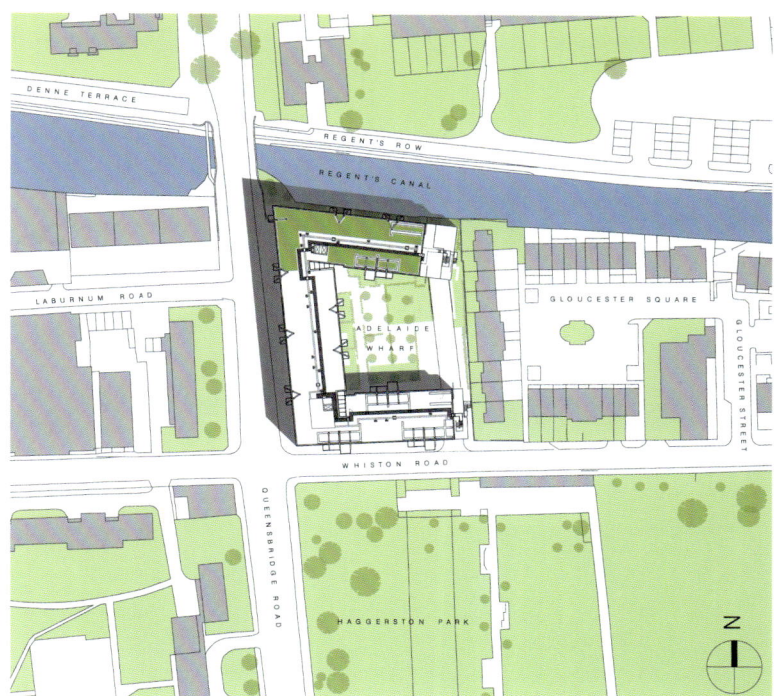

5 | Adelaide Wharf: Plan of the site, located in Hackney, London, adjacent to the Regent's Canal

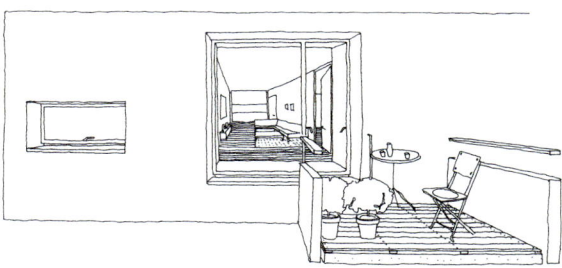

7 | Adelaide Wharf: Proposal sketch, looking back from the balcony into an apartment

6 | 160 Tooley Street: Site location sketch showing entrance and internal street study

Integrated Building Envelope Strategies

types, large and small, that can be modulated across each floor level and up the entire height of the building. |8

Each apartment has a private balcony, hung off beams that are cantilevered from columns projecting through the roof to leave the cladding system clear of penetrations for ease of assembly and construction. The balconies are offset from the windows to allow unobstructed views out, and they are staggered from one story to another to avoid shading the balcony below. This adds an additional pattern of variation to the exterior facade. |9

Construction and Prefabrication

AHMM planned Adelaide Wharf as a simple building mass that could then be clad using an off-site system borrowed from processes used in the design of commercial buildings, where a high degree of flexibility is required for the spaces of primary occupation and more attention to detail is given to "service" elements such as kitchens, bathrooms, and the envelope. The building's massing relies upon the detailed expression of its repeated cladding units to give it a sense of scale and articulation. Planes of different materials within the unitized panels are layered and carefully detailed to give the facade depth and texture.

Building the facade units off-site allowed for lowered costs and construction time, and improved quality control in the details. Prefabrication requires an efficient repetition of elements but can accommodate considerable variation within each panel; this variation was maximized to create interest across the facade. Siberian Larch wood-boards, used for the cladding, alternately overlap and offset each other. The joint between the unitized cladding panels is left visible but goes unnoticed, as it looks the same as the frequently repeated joints between the boards in each panel. The choice of wood boards as a finish was also driven by an aesthetic desire to

9| Adelaide Wharf: Balconies being installed on-site in May 2007

opposite:
8| Adelaide Wharf: Shared landscape courtyard with children's play area in the foreground, overlooked by the staggered window types and the balconies of surrounding apartment units

10| Adelaide Wharf: An unwrapped prefabricated wall panel upon delivery at the site

11| Adelaide Wharf: An inspection of the final cladding's finish and material quality in July 2006

12| Adelaide Wharf: Crane lifting a cladding unit into place

13| Adelaide Wharf: Siberian Larch panels installed on the facade

use a material that would weather and soften over time, and the Siberian Larch wood has low maintenance requirements as well. |10-13

While the unitized system accommodates the repetition of housing units, breaks in the system were emphasized for effect. The main entries and circulation—positioned where the building's grid is broken—allow for the penetration of daylight into stairwells and are articulated by colored vitreous-enamel panelized linings at the entrances. |14

Adelaide Wharf's ground level is built with a more robust, heavyweight brick cladding. This site-built system accommodated for the variations in existing street levels and site edges, and it provides a datum from which the lightweight, unitized system of the higher floors could be installed, thereby protecting it from damage at the sidewalk level. |15

Individual/Collective Identity
Adelaide Wharf is a "tenure blind" development—the whole development has the same facade treatment and collective identity, and there is no differentiation between the varying owner/occupation scenarios. Intense colors are used to give each shared entrance a distinctive address. The balconies have their own color system, so that each unit has an individual identity when viewed from the outside, through a variation of colors along the building.

Metal panels are usually colored with a powder-coating process where color is baked on, like enamel. This is typically a costly operation for small fabrication runs of individual colors, so to economically achieve many colors, AHMM specified the use of Leighs paint, a finish that has no cost premium for small batches of different colors, can easily be touched up on-site, and is very robust—it is even used on North Sea oil rigs. |16

14 | Adelaide Wharf: Vitreous enamel cladding at one of the main entrances on Queensbridge Road

15 | Adelaide Wharf: Brick ground-level entrances, looking north down Queensbridge Road

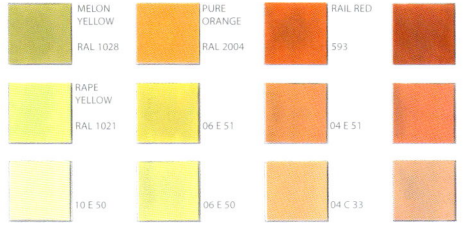

16 | Adelaide Wharf: Balcony color studies

Integrated Building Envelope Strategies

Energy and Light

Housing regulations in the United Kingdom are more concerned with heat loss than solar gain, since residential units tend to have a shallow plan, and therefore have a high wall-to-floor ratio. This drives window sizes down, but it has to be balanced against the daylighting factors required for rooms, which benefit from larger windows. The design target for Adelaide Wharf was for 30 percent glazing, a balance between building-code U-value (rate of heat flow through construction) requirements, cost, and Building Research Establishment (BRE) daylighting guidelines for residential units. While this percentage of glazing is not especially high, the units are perceived as light, open spaces from within, a result of careful window distribution and planning.

Designing Envelopes for Office Spaces: 160 Tooley Street

Program and Urban Context

When design development started on 160 Tooley Street, its location was regarded as marginal—it is wedged between narrow urban side-streets and a raised railway viaduct to the south. |17 This led the project team to consider alternative strategies for the kind of building to be pursued and its likely end users. At an early stage a clear goal was set that 160 Tooley Street should reconsider the commercial office typology, a decision that informed every aspect of the building's design. This new model would be more responsive to issues of sustainability and energy use, and it would work to reconstitute a piece of the city. The need to maximize efficiencies in the building program on a heavily constrained site, coupled with a drive to maximize quality and tackle the issue of materials waste, pointed to a preference for off-site prefabrication of components wherever possible.

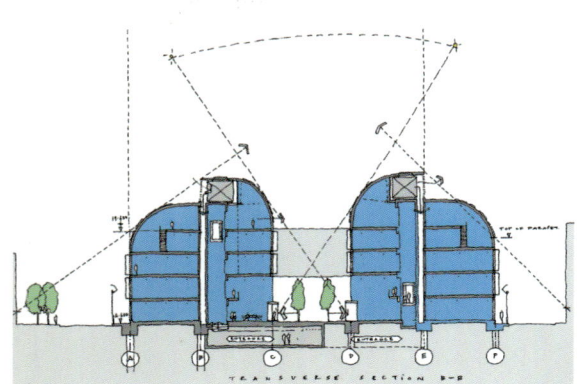

17 | 160 Tooley Street: Design development sketch. The building occupies a dense urban site on the south of Tooley Street in Southwark, and the form and mass of the building were derived from analysis of daylighting requirements as well as a consideration of the characteristics and scale of the surrounding buildings.

Building Envelopes

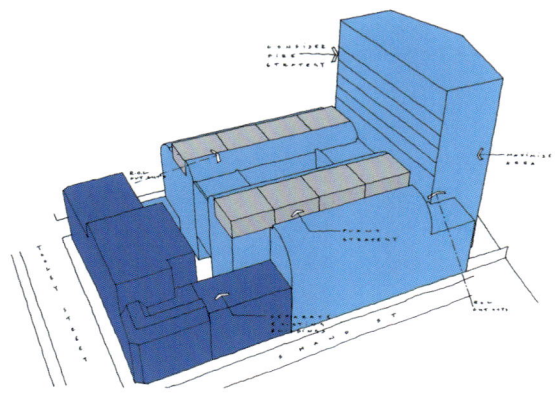

18 | 160 Tooley Street: Early design study looking at building massing (in pale blue) in relation to the surrounding mixed-urban context

19 | 160 Tooley Street: Architect's sketch section exploring ergonomic and environmental comfort factors at the perimeter condition

Integrated Strategy:
Team, Structure, Services, and Envelope

The integration of various contingents of the building team at all stages of the design process was fundamental to 160 Tooley Street's success. Arup acted as both the services and structural engineers, and the contractor was brought into the team six months before construction to work with them and enable on-site coordination. When challenges presented themselves, they were resolved collectively. Every member of the team was driven by to a genuine desire to deliver an outstanding and innovative building.

The simple, precast structural frame of the building and its envelope is a reinterpretation of the massive brickwork construction of existing warehouse buildings adjacent to the site. |18 The structural frame elements—composed of precast slabs with integral reinforcements—were prefabricated and finished in a factory locally before being delivered to the site for assembly with a cast-in-place,

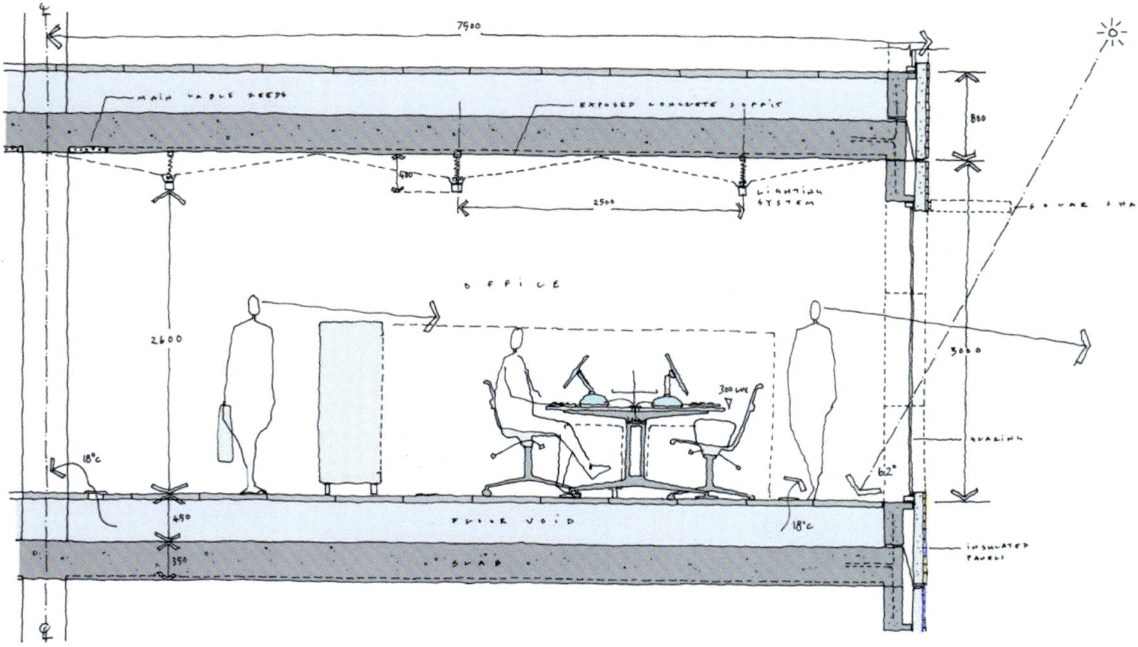

Integrated Building Envelope Strategies

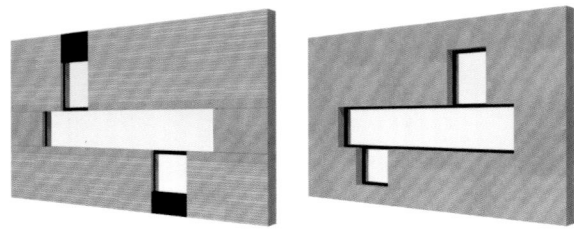
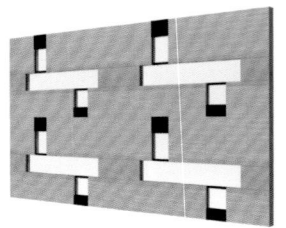
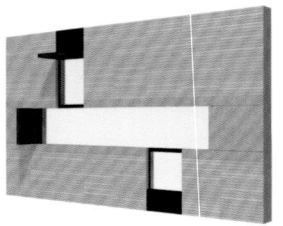

20 | 160 Tooley Street: Early cladding studies

post-tensioned structural top slab. Columns were also prefabricated and clad with precast concrete panels, which allow for a thermal break between structure and envelope. The concrete mixture for the precast cladding units contained mica, which was revealed by light acid etching, giving a sparkle to the building's exterior.

Large-format, high-performance, unitized glazing panels were inserted into this precast structural frame. Their scale—8 x 8 feet (2.4 x 2.4 meters)—reflects the proportions of adjacent buildings, offering views out, good internal daylighting levels, and an enhanced sense of generosity and lightness. |19 The cladding units are articulated with projecting bay windows and solid-colored panels to give the facade depth and shadow when viewed obliquely from the side streets. This system also refines the ratio of clear glazing to opaque areas of the facade, responding to solar-gain load and light levels. |20

A displacement ventilation system is fully integrated with the structure: central columns act as "structural ducts," delivering cooled air from the roof level through a raised floor zone to the perimeter of the building, where the effects of solar heat gain are obviously highest. On average, the facade is 47 percent glazed, ensuring that heat gains, and therefore cooling loads and energy use, are minimized. This is half the percentage of glazing one would expect to see for a typical "glass box" office development.

21| 160 Tooley Street: Barnham Street elevation, connecting spaces through reflection in the external facade glazing

22| Adelaide Wharf: Suspended balconies overlooking Regent's Canal

Inside/Outside

For Adelaide Wharf, the staggering of glazing and solid elements puts the daylight where it is most enjoyed. Rather than obstructing views with a balcony and balustrades, the balcony zone is shifted to the side, avoiding the shading of units below and allowing clear views of the surrounding site and the city from the living spaces.

At 160 Tooley Street, AHMM used large window units to eliminate the typical repeated, "cage-like" 1.5-meter (4.9-foot) mullion module (dictated by standardized office planning grids in the United Kingdom), creating a 1.5 meter/3 meter/1.5 meter (4.9 foot/9.8 foot/4.9 foot) rhythm, and also prevented the wasting of daylight on the carpet below the 750 mm (29.5-inch) desk-height zone. While the architects employed less glass than usual in the building's envelope and it is more solid than a typical office building, its interior actually feels very light and open, because the glass is located where it matters.

In both cases the building envelopes look simple, but they required a high level of coordination between disciplines, a detailed evaluation of daylighting against heat loss, and a strong design sensibility. Building envelope design is as much about the quality of the internal space for building users as it is about an external aesthetic—one cannot be considered without the other. |21-22

Deep Plan

Harlequin 1, BSkyB Transmission and Recording Facility, London, England
Arup Associates

1| Site plan: Harlequin 1 is the largest rectangle, located on the southwest part of the site, adjacent to a dedicated "energy plant farm" that supplies power to the building and forms the base of two large wind turbines. To the northeast of the site are a series of linear buildings that contain other power-supply elements for Harlequin 1, including an energy-efficient combined cooling and heating plant.

Arup Associates, based in London, was founded in 1963 under an initiative directed by the seminal engineer Ove Arup. He wished to formally recognize an organizational structure that had existed within his engineering practice (Ove Arup and Partners), where "architects and engineers work[ed]...on an equal basis...dedicated to the task of improving and reforming...design."[1] Still committed to Ove's vision for holistic "total design," the practice's philosophy has now evolved into what they call "unified design"—a process by which all relevant design decisions are considered together by a well-organized team, making buildings that are a seamless integration of art, technology, and science for the well-being of all who use them.

Arup Associates work from the beginning of any project in tight-knit teams containing architects and structural, building services, and sustainability engineers. Sustainability is at the center of every project by the firm: they are interested in not only simple energy conservation but also a process of "whole life sustainability" that places people first. Whole life sustainability considers how values change in different places, rather than creating models that expect people, cities, and places around the world to behave in identical ways. It looks at sustainability from a wider cultural perspective and incorporates local identity into the design process through a prioritization of human experience, the senses, and memory.

Deep Plan Building

Arup Associates' Harlequin 1 project, located west of London, houses recording, postproduction, and transmission facilities for the European television broadcaster BSkyB. |1 This 230,000-square-foot, four-story building has a footprint with an area roughly equivalent to two New York City blocks. Approximately 330 feet long and 165 feet wide, it includes eight highly unusual naturally ventilated

2| Computer rendering of Harlequin 1, with the giant studio-ventilation chimneys articulated on the exterior to the left

3| The central atrium of the building acts as a large natural ventilation chimney, a circulation space, and as a multipurpose zone for many different social activities, from green-room spaces to recreational facilities.

studios, naturally ventilated offices for 1,370 people, and free-cooled data rooms for more than 400 computer servers. |2

Deep plan buildings have a low ratio of building envelope to floor plate and are often more commercially efficient than narrower building types but require greater mechanical ventilation. At the heart of Harlequin 1 are heavily ventilated, internalized "dark" spaces (spaces that require less natural light than the typical office environment). These dark spaces consist of rack rooms for storing computer servers, specialized postproduction work rooms, and media storage facilities, and they are all located close to the primary service ducts.

Open office space wraps around the dark rooms at the building's core, providing convenient access to them. Equally important, this allows the office areas, where people spend the most time, to be well-lit, naturally ventilated, and to offer good views of the outside. |3 Harlequin 1 is used twenty-four hours a day, and since there are many health problems associated with disturbances of the human circadian rhythm—such as seasonal affective disorder (SAD) and delayed sleep phase syndrome (DSPS)—it was essential to provide its occupants with a relationship to natural day and night cycles.

Eight double-height "floating box" studios are located at the ground-floor level, below the postproduction and office areas, while the top floor houses platform control (where channel content and advertising is monitored and controlled) and more rack rooms, positioned directly below a satellite dish farm. The roof is densely packed with mechanical and electrical equipment.

Building Envelope Sustainability Strategies
Harlequin 1 is a compact, highly efficient, technically driven structure. How does the envelope play a function in the design of the building? As described earlier, there are three major parts to the building:

4 | Harlequin 1 during construction: The studios' natural-ventilation chimneys are aluminum clad, while the studios themselves are double-skinned, "floating" boxes of concrete, visible in the lower portion of the image.

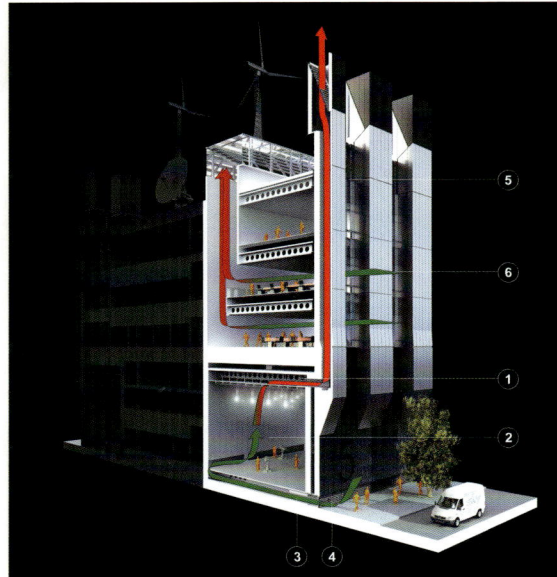

5 | Studio and office natural ventilation diagram:
1. Waste heat from the studio lights rises through the studio-ventilation chimneys.
2. As the waste heat rises, a small negative pressure is created in the studios.
3. This pressure drop overcomes the resistance of the sound attenuators below the studios, drawing in fresh, cool air from the exterior.
4. Exterior intake louvers in the facade allow for outside air to flow through the attenuators and into the studio.
5. When external conditions are inappropriate for natural ventilation, the studio spaces can be mechanically ventilated and cooled using the same chimneys.
6. The offices' internal natural-ventilation chimneys follow principles similar to the studios' chimneys.

technology and equipment components in the central core, "people spaces" wrapped around the core, and recording studios below. Each part has a targeted, task-specific sustainability strategy. The building's core contains "free-cooling" air shafts and other technical components that are not visible from the exterior. However, the passive design strategies for the offices and the soundproof studios are the primary drivers for the envelope design.

Natural Ventilation and Noise Control
The naturally ventilated studios of Harlequin 1 offer a specific technical challenge, as they need to have precise control of external noise. Natural ventilation would appear to work against this: if you open a window, noise is normally brought in, along with the fresh air. Baffles, or attenuators, are required to remove the noise, but the attenuators also restrict airflow.

To overcome the attenuators' resistance, Arup Associates designed a system driven by waste heat given off by the studio lights. Hot air from the lights would usually need to be cooled mechanically, but in this case the hot air is allowed to rise out through giant ventilation chimneys, visible on the exterior of the building. |4 This sets up a pressure differential that draws in cool, fresh external air through sound attenuators in the studios. |5 When weather conditions make natural ventilation inappropriate (when the external temperature is outside of the range of 50-72 degrees Fahrenheit, or 10-22 degrees Celsius), the chimneys can work in reverse to mechanically ventilate and cool the studio spaces. A computerized building management system (BMS) controls internal louvers that can close the natural airflow path and redirect mechanically heated or cooled air into the studios from equipment on the roof of the building.

The giant natural-ventilation chimneys are an integrated component of the facade: they powerfully express the natural ventilation strategy, provide shading to the floor plates of the building, and free up floor space in the interior that would otherwise have been taken up by air-supply systems. The chimneys are clad in aluminum in reference to the machinelike nature of the building, while the studios are clearly articulated on the exterior of the building as double-layered boxes of concrete—one built inside the other, with bearings between to prevent building noise from entering the studios.

Office Space and Envelope

Deep plan buildings are far more difficult to naturally ventilate than their narrow plan counterparts, and they are typically ventilated mechanically. In the case of Harlequin 1, though, Arup Associates used special techniques to ensure that natural ventilation would still be possible. Just as the studios require large chimneys to draw away heat and provide natural ventilation, so too do the office spaces. Their chimneys are integrated into the center of the building, however, and have multiple functions. Not only do the three large internal chimneys draw warm air away from the open offices through the stack effect—they also provide daylight, vertical circulation, and informal meeting spaces. And in an open plan area almost 330 feet long, the chimneys act as wayfinding indicators and help provide a sense of location within the large floor plates.
|6-7 The office's external envelope forms an essential part of the chain of natural ventilation components. It has a number of functions: it lets in natural light and gives access to views, it provides ventilation in a way that allows individuals to feel in control of their environment, and it prevents excessive direct sunlight from overheating the building.
|8 At all levels, Harlequin 1 has high- and low-level, top-hung, motorized-opening windows for natural ventilation. Their airflow principle is similar to that of a sash window, where air can be supplied

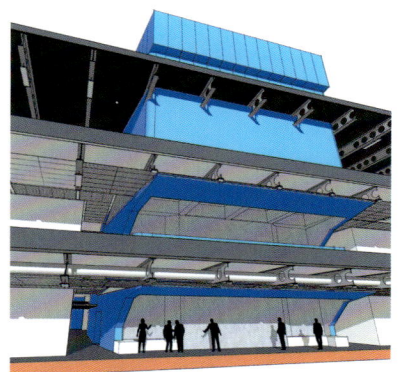

6| A cutaway section through the building shows the central office chimney (in blue), with a multiuse flexible space on the lower level and an atriumlike space above created by a skylight.

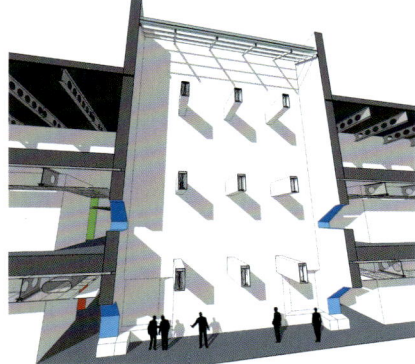

7| This section is taken through the central office chimney, which brings light into the interior of the building and acts as an escape path for warm air.

8| Cutaway section showing the primary components of the offices' envelope from the exterior: studio extract chimneys (1), studio supply ducts (2), natural anodized-aluminum cladding panels (3), and clear and fritted unitized glazing with user/BMS-controlled opening vents (4)

Integrated Building Envelope Strategies

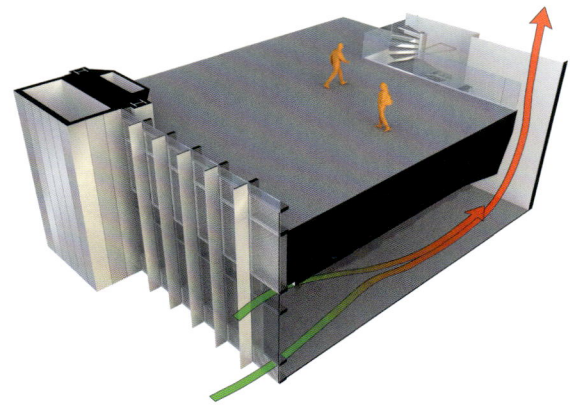

9| Air is drawn in through the envelope's upper and lower top-hung windows, becomes warm within the office floor plates, and escapes upward through the central office-ventilation chimneys.

10| Interior view of an office floor's upper top-hung windows, with the shading fins beyond

11| Exterior view of the shading fins and the upper and lower top-hung windows, with a fritted pattern on the lower windows, which are glazed spandrel panels with louvers behind: The glazed facade of Harlequin 1 is built of unitized cladding elements with extruded, natural anodized-aluminum mullions. The glazing is structural silicone bonded to the carrier frame. Typically, the upper and lower top-hung windows are motor-controlled, opening electronically for natural ventilation.

from either the top or the bottom of the window opening. |9 Windows can be individually opened and adjusted by occupants through the operation of a simple switch on the window itself. This switch glows green on natural ventilation days—days when the BMS has determined that the range of external temperatures are appropriate to naturally ventilate the offices. When the upper or lower limit of this external temperature range is exceeded, the BMS overrides individual control, closes the windows, and implements radiator heating or mechanical cooling as required. In this way, users are given the opportunity to control their own environment, when weather allows. Building studies have demonstrated that this sense of control not only improves the user's experience, it also allows for a wider range of temperatures to be tolerated by the people who use the building—further reducing reliance on mechanical heating and cooling. The final component of the envelope system is its window shading devices, a series of vertical aluminum fins. Arup Associates precisely calculated the fin depths to find the appropriate balance of natural light for each side of Harlequin 1, minimizing heat gain from sunlight that might otherwise penetrate deeply into the building. On the northern elevations, the fins would not be useful, so they were omitted. On the southern elevation, which is most affected by solar radiation, the fins were supplemented with horizontal ceramic fritting that extends entirely across the glass panels. |10-11

Integrated Design and Sustainability
At their heart, television transmission facilities like Harlequin 1 are huge data centers. Worldwide, data centers collectively generate approximately 2 percent of the Earth's carbon emissions annually—double that produced by a country the size of Portugal.[2] Making even small differences to this volume of carbon production will have a positive environmental

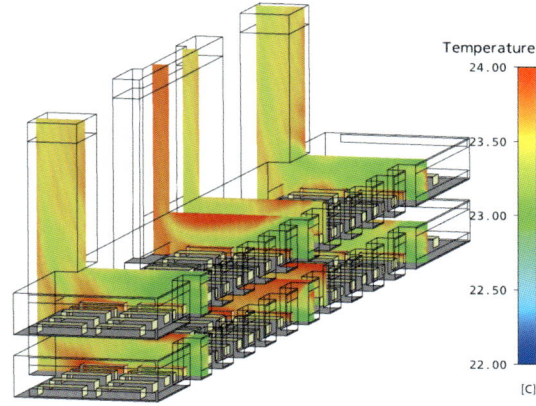

12| During the course of design development, numerous computational fluid dynamic analyses were carried out to demonstrate that the natural ventilation system would be effective. Here, the warm air's path is shown as it flows from the fenestration to the central office chimneys.

13| Photograph of Harlequin 1 under construction in June 2009, from the same perspective as in Figure 1

impact. From the outset, Arup Associates and the client were committed to using every appropriate method to reduce the building's energy profile.

Arup Associates engineers calculated energy use at the beginning of the design process and then tested this continuously throughout the design development period using computational fluid dynamic (CFD) modeling, which simulates how an element such as air or water will behave in a particular space. |12 These analytical methods were essential for deciding the building's orientation, internal spatial configuration, and mechanical systems. The CFD modeling also helped to generate the building's integrated cladding and facade-shading systems, which respond to solar orientation.

The overall architectural result is an unusual building type—the client described it as a "creative factory of ideas," and the local planning authority called it "a new power station architecture for the twenty-first century."[3] The building's envelope is a fundamental expression of clear and entirely integrated sustainability principles, and responds to the possibilities presented by the project's specifics, and not from a preconceived stylistic notion. Every component of the envelope reflects Arup Associates' approach to fully integrated, passive, sustainable design in large-scale, deep plan buildings. Harlequin 1 is the world's most sustainable broadcasting, studio, and data-center building built to date. |13

Feedback Loops

Faculty of English and Institute of Criminology, Cambridge, England
Allies and Morrison Architects

We have developed an understanding of facades as a series of discrete layers, each of which is capable of independent manipulation and control. In part these layers arise as a consequence of the technical performance of the building envelope, a response to the dictates of construction sequence or environmental control. But more importantly they provide the means by which the parallel but sometimes contradictory demands of internal function and external expression are reconciled.

—Bob Allies, "On Building"

When a building is completed, it is usually considered a final product. But completion and handover to the client mark only the start of a building's life. Viewed over thirty years, a building's initial construction budget accounts for just a fraction of its true costs. The primary expenditure over a building's lifetime is likely to be spent on personnel, and their work performance, retention rate, and absenteeism are all highly affected by building comfort. A building's success, therefore, must be considered in the context of its whole life and the comfort and productivity of its users. How can the design process ensure ongoing specific user comfort and performance and sustain appropriate, elegant buildings that anticipate future building program uses and needs?

In 2000, the University of Cambridge commissioned award-winning, London-based architectural practice Allies and Morrison to develop a master plan for its Sidgwick arts and humanities campus and design two new buildings on this campus—the Institute of Criminology and the Faculty of English. |1 The two buildings were completed and occupied in 2004. Four years later, Cambridge's Estate Management and Building Service (EMBS) reviewed the performance of both buildings in terms of user comfort and compared these findings against the original projections of the design team in a post-occupancy evaluation (POE).

1| Master plan drawing of the Sidgwick site, Cambridge, England, 2001: Both rendered in pink, the Faculty of English building is at the top left and the Institute of Criminology at the middle right.

POE reports are carried out to assess how a building is performing after it has been occupied and are vital in helping us understand how well it meets the original intent, the performance expectations, and the ongoing requirements of its users. They offer a constructive way to assess the successes and failures of the projects in terms of performance, comfort, and communication, based on the evaluation of the inhabitants and managers of the building.

Background

The design team was asked to respond to the university's rich historic context, while producing flexible, "future-proof," energy-efficient buildings. In terms of the interiors of the buildings, ease of environmental control and good energy performance took priority, along with psychological and spatial comfort. Development of the designs involved extensive meetings with the buildings' future users in an effort to understand how they occupied their current spaces and what they wanted from their new buildings.

The architects also carefully studied the larger site around the future buildings to help establish a series of sheltered external spaces between them and create clearly articulated "front doors" as part of the campus master plan. This master plan built on the positive aspects of surrounding 1950s buildings—with narrow floor plates and concrete-frame construction—designed by Sir Hugh Casson (of Casson, Conder & Partners), and also considered more recent additions to the site, including James Stirling's Faculty of History (1968), Foster + Partners' Faculty of Law (1996), and Edward Cullinan Architects' Faculty of Divinity (2000). |2-5

Building Envelopes

In addition to providing enclosure, the buildings' envelopes needed to be secure, naturally ventilated,

2| Casson, Conder & Partners' Raised Faculty building in the foreground, with the Institute of Criminology beyond

3| James Stirling's Faculty of History in the foreground, with the south facade of the Faculty of English beyond

4| Edward Cullinan Architects' Faculty of Divinity at far right, Sterling's Faculty of History at slightly to the right of center, and the Faculty of English to the left

5| Foster + Partners' Faculty of Law at left and the Raised Faculty building at right—with a view of the entry to the Institute of Criminology between the two

Integrated Building Envelope Strategies 117

incorporate operable windows, meet high-performance insulation values and air-leakage criteria, and reduce excessive heat gain. Their exterior appearance had to reflect their internal programs while also reconciling broader contextual relationships. The results of these parameters were two very different facade-fabrication systems, each specific to their building, users, and immediate site.

Both buildings use integrated environmental and structural strategies, and they have the same internal office floor area and floor-to-ceiling height. But because each building deals with natural light and air flow in specific ways, the user groups perceive and experience their spaces quite differently. |6-7

6| The main entrance to the Faculty of English, with Stirling's Faculty of History beyond

7| The entry pavilion to the Institute of Criminology, with the threshold to the landscape court

Building Envelopes 118

Criminology, a relatively new discipline, constitutes a branch of the Faculty of Law at Cambridge. Largely composed of postgraduate field researchers, the Institute of Criminology wanted to establish its own distinct identity with their new building. Although most of the department's work requires strict confidentiality and involves interaction with police and government security, researchers wanted the building, and the workspaces, to be light and open. For them, windows were a symbol of progress, transparency, and modern, open thinking. In response, Allies and Morrison's design maximizes areas of clear glazing, which were restricted only by environmental requirements to avoid excessive heat gain in summer and to minimize heat loss in winter. The solid components of the facade are blue-gray, anodized-aluminum panels with white concrete reveals and spandrels that were color-matched to the adjacent Raised Faculty and Faculty of Law buildings. The offices are heated by a perimeter trench heater (which provides convection heat supplied by piped hot water) within the raised floor with vents under each fixed window so that the glazing rises from the finished floor visually unobstructed. |8-9

8| West facade of the Institute of Criminology: The top two floors, which contain offices, have fixed anodized-aluminum panels and louvers (behind which are operable windows), while the library level below has additional areas of glazing behind larger louver panels. Since the lower levels of the building are less exposed to heat gain (due to overshadowing) and also house the more public library, the building becomes more transparent from top to ground level.

9| Diagram showing the relationships between the windows, columns, and walls of the Institute of Criminology: Circular columns sit inboard of the facade and are offset from the internal partition grid so that a partition never clashes with a column—unlike in the Faculty of English building, where the square columns are aligned with the partition grid. It was established early in the briefing process that the English faculty would be far less likely to change their internal layout, whereas Criminology required greater flexibility to reconfigure depending on the research work and teams within the department.

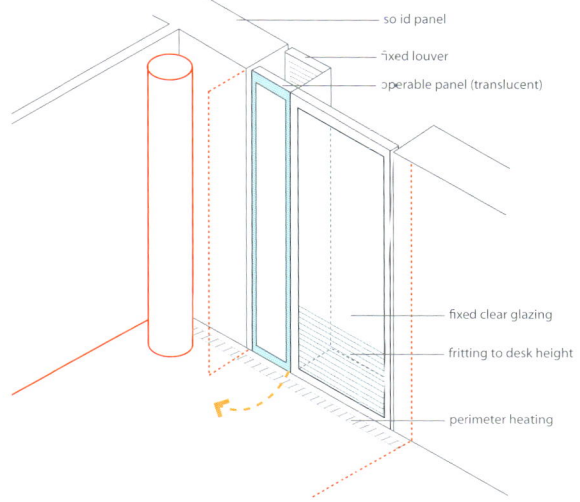

Integrated Building Envelope Strategies

In contrast, the priority for members of the English Faculty was to be able to teach their largely undergraduate student body in small groups around a private study table. Their building is organized as a series of individual rooms arranged along corridors, with a facade articulated by "punched" openings—windows framing the world beyond for each faculty member and associated student group. The cladding material is a warm-colored, terra-cotta rain-screen system in reference to the famous red brick of the adjacent Faculty of History building. The offices in this building are heated by more-visible, wall-mounted panel radiators placed below each window, where one might sit to read a book. |10-11

While recognizing the need to give each building a unique identity to suit its current use, EMBS was mindful of commissioning buildings that could also serve future needs—even those that were not yet apparent. The briefs for both the English and Criminology buildings called for as much flexible space as possible—more in line with commercial office "shell and core" developments. Both buildings, while identifying specific office spaces, allow for partitions to be removed or added, based on a 1.5 meter module (a standard metric planning

10| East facade of the Faculty of English: Each window aligns directly with an office space behind. The "punched" openings, with fixed glazing and an asymmetrical operable window behind fixed louvers, are surrounded by a terra-cotta panel rain-screen system.

11| Diagram showing the relationships between the windows, columns, and walls of the Faculty of English: The face of each square concrete columns aligns with the partition grid, so that where a partition occurs the face of the internal wall is flush with the column face on one side and projects into the adjacent office on the other.

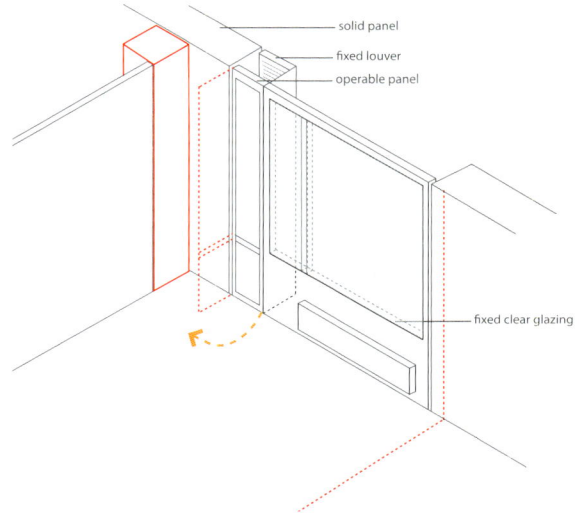

Building Envelopes   120

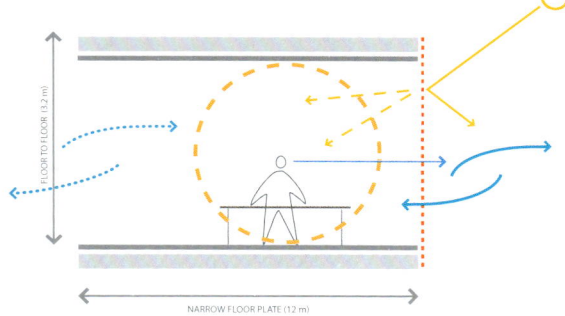

12 | The office design for both buildings focused on user comfort: view, air, noise control, and temperature.

Space type	% of average higher education campus	Electrical target (kWh/year)	Fossil target (kWh/year)
Teaching	25	22	151
Research	20	105	150
Lecture hall	5	108	412
Office	30	36	95
Library	10	50	150
Catering	2.5	650	1100
Recreational	7.5	150	360
Total academic	100 of academic (75% of total)	75	185
Residential	100 of residential (25% of total)	85	240

13 | This government chart showing annual target energy-consumption figures (in a typical higher-education campus) for representative space types is used as a base reference by Estate Management and Building Service at the University of Cambridge.

dimension, equivalent to 4.9 feet). Areas of glazing are balanced to allow good levels of daylight but still restrict additional solar heat gain or loss. Glazing dimensions are also governed by the internal planning grid, making it easier to divide internal space in the future and still have access to an operable window in every room. The relationship between windows for light and ventilation, structure, heating systems, potential internal planning, and control are inextricably linked. |12

Structural and Environmental Integration
As part of their integrated design and environmental strategy, the design team implemented a heavyweight concrete-frame construction in both buildings to "naturally modulate the temperature of internal spaces, absorbing excess heat during the daytime and releasing it at night through large areas of exposed thermal mass."[1] The architects designed the high-performance building envelopes to reduce thermal loss above and beyond the requirements of building codes and, with effective shading, allow for larger glazed areas, resulting in good levels of daylighting throughout.

Rather than attempting to achieve a steady, constant temperature at all times, the project's environmental engineers, Buro Happold, noted that "by keeping in the recommended comfort bands, the internal temperature [of the buildings] should be allowed to swing with the external temperature over a twenty-four-hour cycle by using the thermal mass of the building. This will ensure that the active systems are kept to a minimum."[2] Maximum comfortable temperatures for the buildings' offices and library spaces were studied and tested extensively using building simulation software. Actual energy-data output from the last two years has shown that both buildings are consistently on target with, or close to, the recommended performance levels for electricity consumption. |13

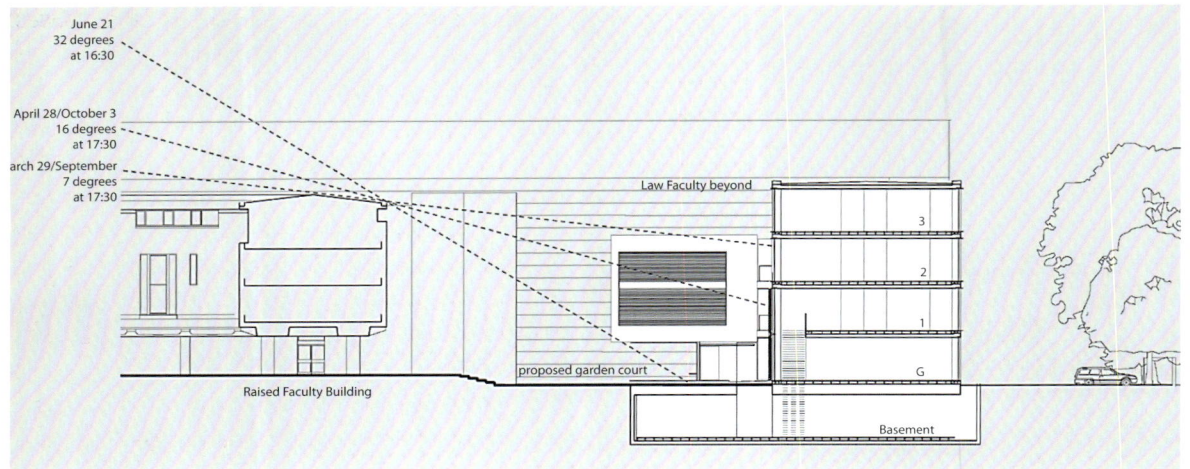

14| Sun angles on the west facade of the Institute of Criminology, at the equinox and solstices

15| Interior view of a Faculty of English study space

Comfort and Control

POE reports for both buildings, in the form of building-user feedback, have shown no negative accounts regarding solar heat gain or glare, both of which were a concern for the design team since the buildings have predominantly east- and west-facing facades. |14 A computer-based building management system (BMS) controls and monitors the internal environments of the buildings, including heating and artificial lighting, but users have complete and direct control of blinds and operable windows. Research has generally shown that, given the option, people will open a window to help cool themselves via increased air flow.[3] Even if this does not always help to actually cool a space, it does offer a perceived level of comfort, and generally people will tolerate higher internal temperatures if they have control over operable windows. |15

Communication: Design and Operation

An institutional building's design has to go through rigid, and often complex, sign-off processes at each stage of its development. However, there is frequently a gap between a building's designed performance as intended by the architects and its actual day-to-day operations management.

Building Envelopes 122

16 | Interior view of the Institute of Criminology's faculty common room, looking to the west facade beyond

17 | Interior view of the Faculty of English's ground-level common room

Communication, together with a clear process, was vital in terms of enabling successful design progress, systems integration, maintenance, and user education with these two buildings. Where there were communication gaps in the design process is invariably where problems have arisen with the day-to-day use of the buildings. Likewise, resolution was most comprehensive where the right parties were brought together at key moments.

In theory, an institutional facility, as a long term owner occupier, has perhaps the greatest potential to achieve maximum integration and energy performance through design, specification, management, user education, and a vested interest in return. Over the life of an institutional building, responsibility must be shared between the creators of the initial briefing, the design team, the contractors, the commissioning team, the client, and building managers and users. Successful and well-integrated passive design especially requires not only a proactive client and design team but also engaged occupants, given succinct and clear building-operating instructions (for example, annual or even seasonal reminders of how and when to open and close windows to enable the optimum performance of a natural ventilation strategy) that can then be supported by sophisticated building management systems, now commonly specified for buildings of this type, and well-trained facilities managers.

In formal terms, detailed attention to the relationships between building grids, structure, environmental strategies, siting, and concept, right through to manufacture and assembly of materials, all play a part in "distilling complex issues of modern construction into well-designed and integrated buildings."[4] However, user behaviors and their influence over a building's design and day-to-day operation are, and continue to be, an active determinant in energy performance and comfort, pre- and post-occupation. |16-17

Integrated Building Envelope Strategies

Plug-ins

Tooley Street Terrace, London, England
Hawkins\Brown Architects

opposite
1| The New Biochemistry building at the University of Oxford (2008) is an example of a project by Hawkins\Brown that addresses the sensitive intervention of a new building with an existing one—in this case, a new academic building adjacent to the Pitt Rivers Museum in Oxford.

Building envelopes generated by the studio Hawkins\Brown are not seen as a self-contained, two-dimensional exercise. They are considered as a complex component of a building's DNA and are generated holistically, along with the concepts and principles of the entire building. The firm conceives of building envelopes as complex filters or expressions of threshold that mediate climatically, compositionally, and culturally and help to define a building's place in a civic or social context. Each envelope that Hawkins\Brown develops and generates for a project becomes as unique as its context, client, orientation, and program. Much of the practice's work has dealt with the creative and adaptive reuse of existing buildings, and many of the strategies that they have developed for new buildings have come from working in this context. |1

Urban Fabric
The Tooley Street Terrace project was developed as part of a master plan conceived by the firm Foster + Partners, in a development called More London, close to Tower Bridge and the riverfront on the south side of the Thames, where the new Foster-designed Greater London Assembly building now sits. An existing terrace (a row of connected buildings) located along Tooley Street, at the southeasternmost corner of the More London area, was one of the last remaining plots of the master plan to be developed. |2 The terrace buildings are within a historic conservation area and were to remain as a fragment of the streetscape of the former neighborhood, which was once a warehouse area for goods storage adjacent to the Thames.

Although this project was a speculative office commission, it presented a complex design challenge that required "plugging in" to the existing fabric: housing and small-scale commercial buildings to the south (the neighborhood of North Bermondsey) and master-planned offices to the

Integrated Building Envelope Strategies

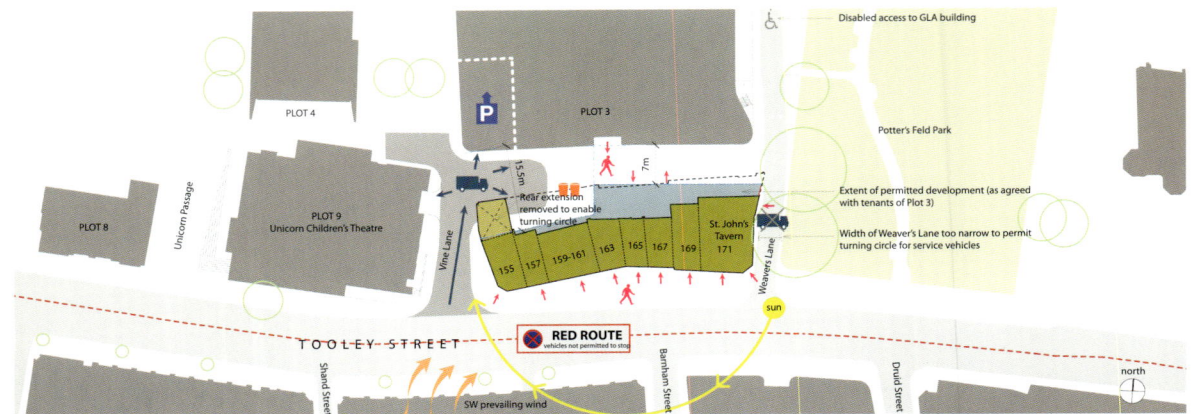

2 | Tooley Street Terrace site plan, illustrating the relationship between the terrace and the surrounding buildings within the More London development

north (part of the More London development). Hawkins\Brown's proposal mediated between and joined together the emerging More London development with North Bermondsey, not only physically but also in its purpose and social context. The firm had to allow flexibility in their building design for multiple occupancy scenarios while also making the project place-specific.

Tooley Street Terrace accommodates small-scale retail space at its ground floor, then has three floors above with fifteen thousand square feet of flexible and adaptable studio/office space—all behind a mix of existing, refurbished, and new facades. The "bookends" of Tooley Terrace—St. John's Tavern and the Antigallican—were once hostelries, a combination of pub and lodging that held cultural importance for the people who had lived and worked in the area. The architects refurbished St. John's Tavern to accommodate a bar/cafe/restaurant, and it is hoped that it will remain a social gathering place for the neighborhood.

Stitching

A very detailed analysis of the structural conditions and historic values of the existing facades was undertaken to determine which elements were important to retain or contributed to the townscape setting of the terrace, and which were

Building Envelopes   126

3 | Photomontage, giving a street elevation view of Tooley Street Terrace's context

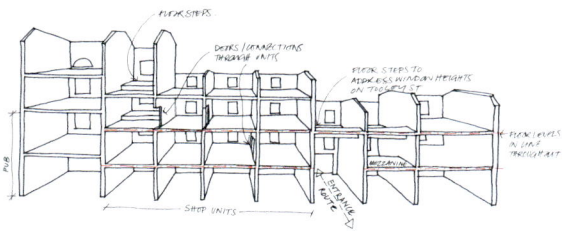

4 | Floor-level resolution sketch, showing how the complicated arrangement of floor levels within the original terrace of buildings was addressed for adaptive reuse

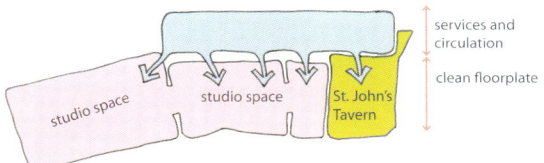

5 | Concept sketch, illustrating the relationship between the service and vertical-circulation zone (in blue), the office/studio floor plates (in pink), and the self-contained bar/restaurant (in yellow)

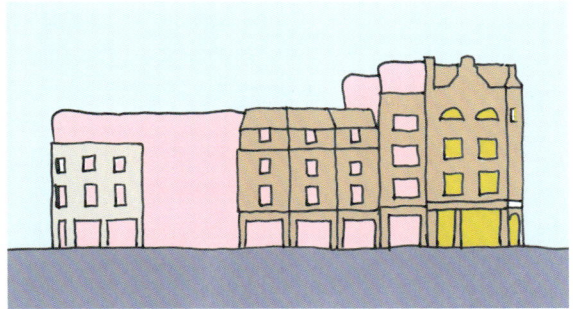

6 | Facade concept sketch, with area of new construction rendered in pink

beyond reasonable repair. Hawkins\Brown considered the collection of buildings on the site as a whole, and their building envelope design responds to the entire 360-degree outlook from the site. |3 Many elements of the preexisting terrace buildings have been retained, and the firm's early, detailed studies ensured that the most important historical fabric was kept and that, where buildings were removed, new elements of structure would exert a presence onto the main elevation of the terrace, heralding a dynamic new life for the terrace and its surrounding context.

Tooley Street Terrace is made up of a number of individual structures whose floor levels (due to their differing ages) are not aligned with each other. Hawkins\Brown, working with the structural engineers Adams Kara Taylor, investigated a number of different floor-level configurations to establish a structural datum for each floor while also making an efficient floor-to-ceiling height. |4 This was balanced against the need to fabricate consistent and cost-effective facade components that would be repeatable as much as possible vertically throughout the building. By reconfiguring floor levels and providing a new circulation and service element—containing elevators, stairs, bathrooms, and vertical service risers—to the rear, Hawkins\Brown reorganized the collection of buildings into a single whole while retaining their individual characters. |5-6

Facade

The concept for Tooley Street Terrace's facade was inspired by a parlor game of lifting a teacup with a balloon without touching the cup. The preexisting

7| Balloon and teacup concept image, with the existing buildings on-site as the teacup and the new construction as the balloon

8| Detail of the north facade, illustrating the solid anodized-aluminum panels and the transparent and colored glass windows, which have a ceramic frit applied to mask the floor/ceiling zone

terrace is analogous to the tea cup as a "host," with the balloon being represented by the new intervention, pressing itself against the host's existing structure and exerting its presence without overwhelming the host. |7 The new intervention is partially visible through the existing elevations, contributing to the concept of the historic buildings as a host. Hawkins\Brown intended for the old and new building elements to complement each other and to have an engaging presence on the new streetscape. The materials for the new elements within the scheme were carefully selected to respond to the new composition while respecting the historic buildings of the terrace.

The new facade is a flush-unitized glazed system, whose large-scale framed cladding units were prefabricated with a combination of glass and anodized-aluminum panels off-site and then installed in a seemingly irregular pattern. |8 The spacing of the glazing mullions was generated from the existing terrace buildings' window configurations and the massing of surrounding adjoining buildings. The rhythm established within the new building envelope along Tooley Street continues around to the rear of the building. A material change from glass to more solid, insulated, anodized-aluminum panels occurs to identify the change in buildings between 155-169 and 171 St. John's Tavern, but the established rhythm is maintained. The facade becomes more transparent as it wraps around the building to the north, with glazing forming the majority of the elevations to the south and north, thus maximizing the light within the flexible workspaces and offering a degree of transparency through the building.

The unitized facade system consists of a combination of clear and colored glass with varying degrees of transparency, achieved through the deployment of fritting to disguise floor and ceiling interfaces and transparent colored-film interlayers, which offer visual warmth and character. Hawkins\

9 | Color studies for Tooley Street Terrace's building envelope, taken from the surrounding neighborhood

Brown developed the color palette by "sampling" from the colors of the buildings and environment of Tooley Street and the surrounding More London development. |9 A number of color studies of varying intensity and distribution were prepared and tested within the studio to understand the effects of colored light within a workspace. Much consideration was given to the final selection of colored glazing, ensuring that the warmth of the predominant umber and red colors were balanced with a blue-green glass.

This poetic use of colored glass is combined with a pragmatic application in response to resolving solar gains and providing shading for the interior. Since much of the south facade consists of the brick of the original terrace, new insertions of glass could be added, carefully balancing heat gains with daylight levels. The color of the facade is at its most intense on the prominent south-facing elevation and dissipates as it wraps around the building. The use of color in the building emphasizes and enhances the playful presence, scale, and character of the terrace. At night, the combination of lighting and color acts as a beacon along Tooley Street, signaling the regenerated building and celebrating its new life. |10

10 | Elevation drawings, showing the ratio of solid to void and the distribution of colored glass on the facade

Control

Hawkins\Brown used a mixed-mode strategy to deal with air circulation and climate control in the building: natural ventilation is supplied through operable windows. The firm prefers to employ simple methods of environmental control wherever possible to ensure that building users can easily understand the ways to adapt and modify their environment—opening a window when you are hot or purging stale air at night. The temperate

London climate and the depth of Tooley Street Terrace's plan make this possible for much of the year. The project's environmental engineers, RHB Partnership, tested the building's performance extensively to keep the climate-control strategy as simple as possible. The building's raised floor zones and service-space allowances enable the system to be enhanced if required by the tenant. For example, if air-conditioning is required because an office plan becomes highly compartmentalized or has heavy computer use, then it is possible to install comfort cooling. However, air-conditioning is not available as a default system, reducing capital costs, carbon emissions, and ongoing energy expenses.

Inside Out, Outside In
Often, facades are considered solely as the external skin or face of a building, but Hawkins\Brown see them as the edge of interior architecture and a vessel for activity inside a building. The firm tests facade designs to understand and respond to the needs of two often conflicting conditions: what it's like to be inside looking out, as well as outside looking in. They also seek to address a fundamental question: How are the inhabitants nurtured?

Tooley Street Terrace was not developed for a specific occupant, but still the quality of space and the kind of environment it offers was carefully considered in terms of occupation. The firm thoughtfully articulated the relationship between old and new and used color as an uplifting quality that constantly recalibrates time throughout the space. |11

Working with historic buildings requires a careful hand and an open, enquiring, responsive approach. Buildings have their limitations, but they also allow opportunities for change or intervention. Understanding an existing built condition makes us able to respond pragmatically as well as dynamically, to see and seize the creative opportunities as well as to respond to "as-found" conditions. |12

11 | Interior view of sunlight coming in through the colored glass

12 | Exterior view at nighttime from Tooley Street, with the More London development in the background

Integrated Building Envelope Strategies

Maximizing Value

290 Mulberry Street, New York, New York
SHoP Architects

1| 290 Mulberry Street site plan

What constitutes value in good design? For "green" design, a market cachet has been easier to quantify, since it can bring direct dollars-and-cents benefits such as lower cost over lifecycle, tax incentives, and better internal quality for occupants, not to mention the social benefit of helping the environment. However, the matter of good design value in other senses is harder to assess. Two types of value in design come first from a responsibility to the clients, who need to understand that they are getting value that will be realized economically, and second from a responsibility to a place's inhabitants, who require good design to bring social and experiential value to the building they occupy.

SHoP Architects have crafted a specific type of value in their New York practice: they work in a very pragmatic way that has resulted in a uniquely entrepreneurial, yet poetic approach. While they were one of the first practices to move digital technology out of imaging and into tectonics, their practice is not defined by digital design. SHoP uses ingenuity, creativity, and technology to leverage good design without adding cost for the client. They have utilized the potentials of digital design and fabrication to yield economics in construction, but not at the expense of design quality or value.

Context
Located at the northwestern edge of the NoLIta (North of Little Italy) area of New York City, 290 Mulberry Street is bound on the north by Houston Street and on the west by the historic Puck Building on Mulberry Street. |1 The building is thirteen stories high, including a mechanical penthouse, with commercial space located at the ground floor and cellar and a total of nine residences above. Its typical floor plate is only two thousand square feet. Considering the value of real estate in the area, optimization of 290 Mulberry Street's exterior-enclosure depth was critical in reaching a balance

2| The corner of the Puck Building, with 290 Mulberry in the foreground during construction

3| Drawing articulating the building envelope code analysis

between value added through building envelope design and a return on sellable space.

A zoning district requirement specifying a "predominantly masonry" enclosure for the two sides of the building facing Houston and Mulberry created an opportunity to respond directly to the Puck Building—one of New York's most recognizable masonry buildings. |2 Consequently, the project is defined by its context and is a direct response to zoning and building code regulations. SHoP's design concept focused on the interpretation of local laws and regulations with a contemporary response to masonry construction and detailing that avoids pastiche.

Making a Problem into a Possibility
The design of 290 Mulberry Street was driven by multiple key criteria: maximizing internal area, staying within the allowable facade projection limit as defined by code, and minimizing the overall depth of the building's envelope. When coupled with material properties and fabrication constraints, these requirements began to define an approach that was a contemporary reinterpretation of brick detailing.

Advancements in building technology have allowed for ever-thinner wall construction, with high demand and limited buildable areas adding financial pressure to this trend. However, it is the thickness of traditional masonry facades that allows for their layered, decorative ornamentation. With no technical requirement for a thick wall, and with financial pressure to not take up sellable area inside the property line, SHoP looked for allowable space outside the site's property line to create contemporary ornamental reliefs. New York City building code allows ten square feet over any given one hundred square feet of a building's enclosure to project beyond the property line, by up to ten inches. This allowance was written with extruded ornament such as bullnoses and cornices in mind.

Integrated Building Envelope Strategies

4| Single prefabricated brick-panel unit, before shipment to the site

5| Rendered view looking north on Mulberry Street to show the building's wrapped brick facade and concrete inner core

SHoP came up with a "rippled" design for the building envelope—with bricks stacking incrementally in a field condition over the entire surface (as opposed to a singular element sticking out, like a bullnose)—which did not fit within the context imagined by building code. The "valley" of the ripple occurs at the property line, so almost 100 percent of the facade is beyond the property line, if only by as little as three-quarters of an inch. Using analytical software to diagram the average degree of extension beyond the property line, SHoP was able to secure a variance to the building code. |3

The envelope's pattern, in which every brick is stepped in precise increments, could not have been achieved by masons laying the bricks by hand on-site. Instead, the bricks were fabricated at a factory into custom precast panels. |4 In addition to allowing for design flexibility, panelized construction tends to have higher quality control, since it is factory produced, and has the schedule benefits of off-site fabrication—panels can be fabricated while the building's structure is being erected, and then brought to the site and installed very quickly with a crane. This minimizes the time it takes to enclose a building, which is critical to beginning interior and finish work.

The architects were able to achieve maximum effect and additional square footage at a minimum cost by utilizing digital fabrication technology. The building envelope of 290 Mulberry Street is an incredibly textured, street-facing wrapper over a simple, concrete-frame inner core. The proportion of window to solid wall is roughly the same as a tenement building (the predominant housing type in the surrounding neighborhood), but the whole building envelope is clearly articulated with a series of staggered, punched windows. The envelope's "wrapper" concept and rigorous use of brick give a sense of unity to the whole, while the window openings and unit panels create a more dynamic visual impact and differentiate this as a contemporary facade. |5

Evolution of Intent through Implementation
Fabrication and constructability concerns caused the design development stage to progress at two different scales concurrently. At a small scale, individual bricks could not protrude past any of their neighbors by more than three-quarters of an inch. Equally important was making sure that the overall coursing of the panels worked together with the column spacing, floor-to-floor heights, and window openings. Through the use of different design models, both physical and digital, SHoP developed the design through a bottom-up process that concerned itself with brick placement, and a top-down process focused on panel design. |6-8

The architects conceived of the building envelope as a process of layering, rather than considering it as a stand-alone, preconceived form—they began parametric digital modeling of the envelope before they knew what the building would look like. Parametric modeling specifically enables the investigation of potential components and fabrication techniques, based on given parameters or constraints rather than an inherent geometry, so the constraints could be defined and the design process could evolve knowing that all the parameters were being taken into account and not inhibiting possibility.

Feedback Loops and Testing
The implementation of varied software applications at different stages of 290 Mulberry Street's process enabled design feedback loops that both tested and affirmed technological and aesthetic design decisions within specific parameters. The architects utilized the best tools for each part of the process in an open-platform, multi-device approach. The separation of digital modeling

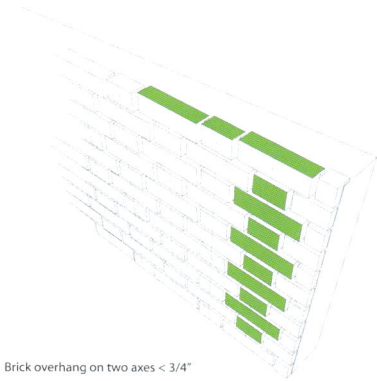

Brick overhang on two axes < 3/4"

6| Drawing of the brick facade's Flemish bond pattern

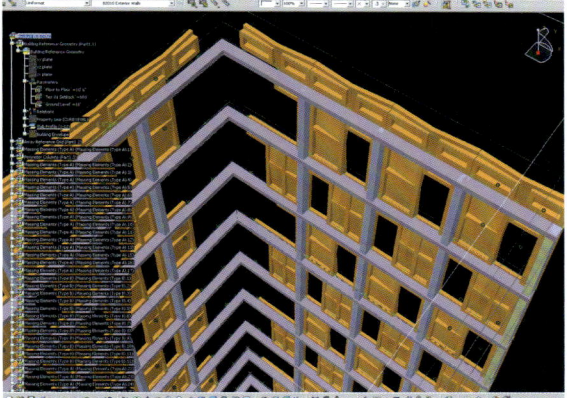

7| Computer model of the envelope, showing coordination of the structure with window locations and panel design

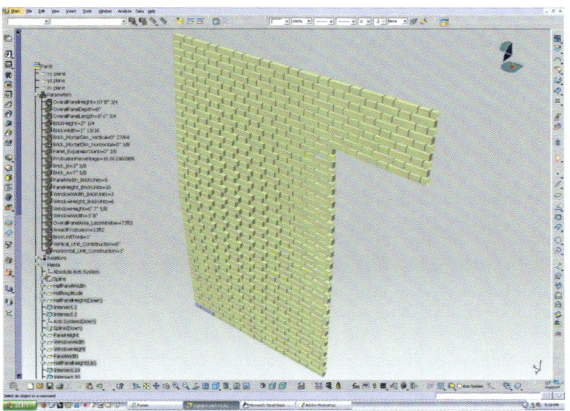

8| Parametric model controlling layout of each brick within a panel

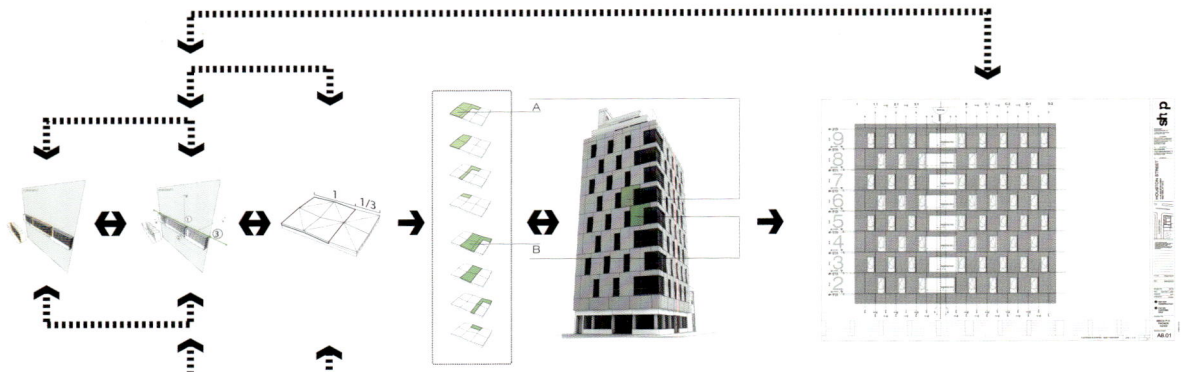

9 | Diagram of 290 Mulberry Street's feedback-loop design process, showing how each scale of operation informed the others

10 | CNC fabrication of the "master" positive, from which rubber liners are created

tools served a key role in quality control, as every model was used as an opportunity to double-check the project's data and geometries. |**9** The software allowed the firm to set up simple rules quickly, test them, and change them immediately. This platform was both clear and precise, yet open enough to support a design process that was in constant flux.

This project was the first to test and implement a building information modeling (BIM) platform within the office. BIM is a software technology allowing information such as component quantities and properties to be embedded in a digital model, which automatically correlates changes made in any model view to all associated parts of the model. SHoP produced the building documents using Revit, a BIM software allowing parametric association between all components, from panel geometry data generated from various other software programs.

Dialogue

The materiality and fabrication of the brick panels were integral to the building envelope's design and a driving factor from the start. Because of this, SHoP brought in the fabricator and cladding contractor at the earliest possible stage to work on fabrication techniques and achieve the construction tolerances required within, and between, panels.

11| Casting the rubber liners, used to make each of the envelope's unitized panels

12| A rubber liner unit, which holds each individual brick in place for the fabrication of the panels

13| Bricks being placed in the liner: The back surfaces of the bricks are keyed to form a mechanical attachment with the concrete layer.

14| An in-process panel with formwork surround in place, bricks in the liner, and steel reinforcement bars on top, prior to concrete pour

Integrated Building Envelope Strategies

15 | Drawing showing the variety of panel types that were created from a single master positive form: Since the master is expensive to fabricate, a main objective of the design was to generate all the required panel types from one form.

The key to the envelope's panel fabrication is in the form liner that was used to hold the bricks in place within each panel's form while its concrete backing was being cast. This liner, a flexible rubber, was produced from an original positive that was milled from files produced by SHoP, working with the fabricator, Saramac. |10-14 Because of the high cost of fabricating the original milled element, SHoP designed liners for every panel in the enclosure system to be cast from a single master of the smallest possible size. |15 The use of this master to the maximum changed the way every detail of the building envelope was resolved: panel to panel, window unit to panel, brick to concrete, and panel to steel structure. The research and development that went into the accurate testing of the construction process mostly focused on the liner. Each brick's placement, its relationship to its neighbors, and the form given to the mortar joints were all controlled through this component, so accurate fabrication of the liner was critical.

Value and Economy
Through 290 Mulberry Street's design development process, an ingenious logic of simple form evolved. The building's design has a rigorous economy, achieved through the imposed parameters of value. This project is not about the implementation of digital technology as a tool but rather about the architects' integrated approach to computer software, which frames design possibilities both technically and aesthetically—with economical and beautiful results.

The integration of a building's envelope, structure, and services on-site is often the most complex part of its construction process, and it is also where failure is most likely to occur during the life of the building. The real benefit of BIM in this project and others is its potential to bring the design and construction teams together at the

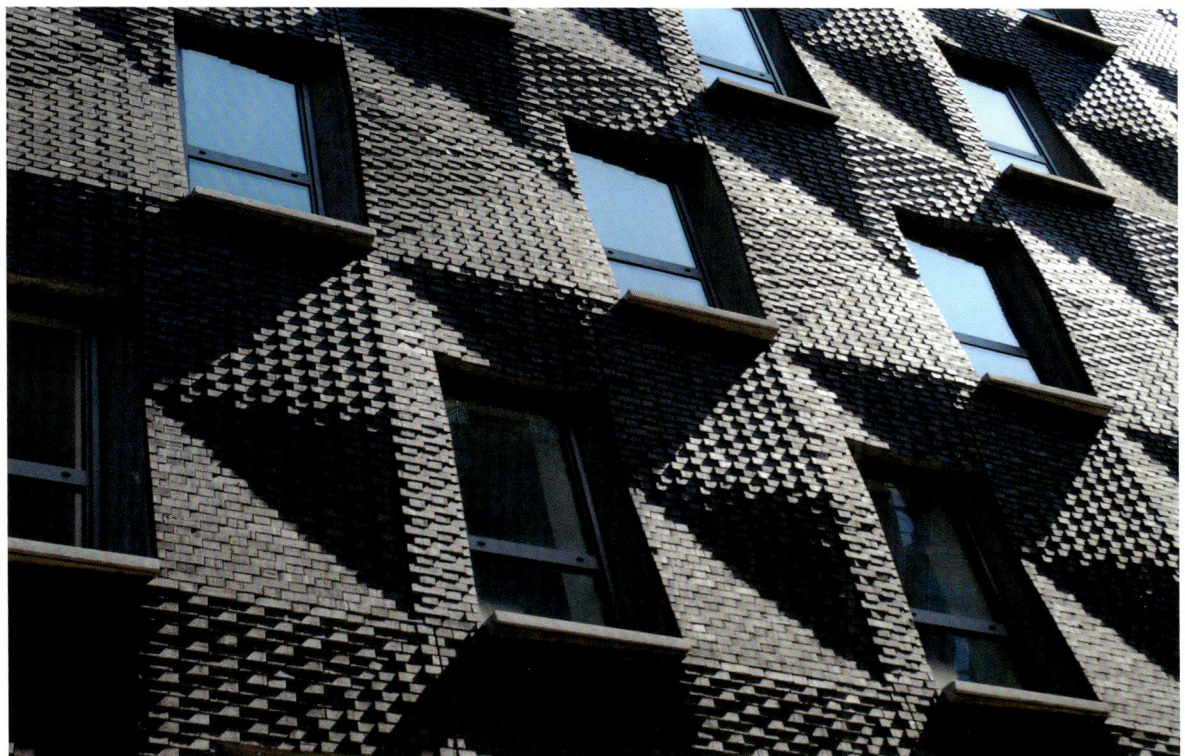

16| View of 290 Mulberry Street's completed facade

very earliest stages of design development. This allows them to solve problems before they ever happen on-site, integrating design components in the present virtually rather than troubleshooting them later and maximizing possibility and potential to bring ultimate value. |16

Made to Measure

The Charlotte Building Offices, London, England
Lifschutz Davidson Sandilands

It has often proven more cost-effective to design a bespoke, job-specific solution that is optimized and efficiently meets the required performance criteria. Unnecessary components that provide redundant flexibility may be omitted, with consequent savings to the contract. Innovation, where necessary, is based upon a careful consideration of precedents to generate appropriate solutions tested to verify their performance.

—Andrew Hall, Arup facade engineer

1| A curved corner of the Charlotte Building Offices as built

Lifschutz Davidson Sandilands is a London-based architectural and design practice with a wide range of work. They understand and control each project's design and construction process, budget, and program with a commitment to context and an attention to detail. The firm approached their custom-made building envelope for the Charlotte Building, a new speculative office construction in London's West End, with an aspiration to exceed technical expectations and delight with a simple, clear design. |1

There are many reasons why a bespoke, or made-to-measure, facade might be employed for a particular project: the site context and constraints, technical and aesthetic considerations, the aspirations of the client, or a combination of all these factors and more. The Charlotte Building's complex design and technical brief, its busy site, and the market demands of prospective tenants (the building is located in a high-end area of London where many advertising agencies and such are based) all meant that an "off-the-shelf" building would not be possible, so Lifschutz Davidson Sandilands developed a bespoke building envelope system for it. |2

Context and Appearance
The building is sited within a historically significant area of the West End characterized by eighteenth- and nineteenth-century buildings, many of masonry construction with smaller window openings, and it was important that the new building relate to this

2| Computer rendering of the corner facing the courtyard off Gresse Street: The curved glazing panels are key to achieving a "taut skin" aesthetic. The sloped external ground level is accommodated with angled sill profiles that match the slope and a black glass spandrel concealing the floor void behind.

Integrated Building Envelope Strategies

3| Site plan and identification of the key site constraints that the Charlotte Building Offices address

legend:
— site boundary
...... ownership boundary
— borough boundary
▢ Hanway Street Conservation Area

4| The facade during installation, showing the construction sequence in horizontal bands starting from the ground floor

existing context in terms of its facade articulation and the proportions of its fenestration. |3 While clients and tenants often desire an archetypal, all-glass office building, the constraints of sensitive contexts, as well as increasingly demanding environmental legislation in the United Kingdom in terms of energy use, mean that this is increasingly challenging to realize in new buildings.

While the project demanded a contextual response, it was important that the final building achieve a modern and contemporary aesthetic. The firm designed the seven-story office building with a richness of detail at all scales. Along the facade at each floor level, they employed a double-glazed, fritted spandrel with an anodized-aluminum backing to reduce the percentage of clear glazing on the facade while maintaining a taut glass-skin aesthetic. |4-5 The white-dotted fritting pattern on the glazed "shadow box" spandrels creates a dynamic texture that varies with the changing play of light against the surface. |6 Gold and natural-colored anodized aluminum, black fritted glass, and stainless steel were also used on the envelope's exterior.

Advance Procurement

The scale and complexity of the scheme presented a challenge to the procurement of the facade. Projects such as the Charlotte Building fall between two categories: too large for production by small artisan manufacturers and too small to be economically viable for the larger cladding contractors. Such buildings can be difficult to bid as custom packages in the United Kingdom, and it was therefore important to adequately market-test the project at an early stage to ensure viability. This drove the decision to pre-procure a contractor for the facade in advance of the main contract to obtain cost certainty and validate the bespoke approach.

The long production schedule associated with the technical design and fabrication of custom

5| A unitized panel prototype used for the Centre for Window and Cladding Technology testing (not installed on the building)

6| Sheets of the fritted glass for the spandrel panels, stacked up in the factory

facades also favors an early procurement, because it can facilitate a more rapid start on-site and does not require a main contractor to have been appointed. Although the detailed design of the cladding must be resolved earlier in the design process than normal to allow for an early bid, this strategy promotes the integration of the facade's technical design with the whole building.

Integration and User Comfort

From a technical point of view, the Charlotte Building's services and environmental strategy were substantial design drivers in terms of the facade configuration, requiring solar heat gains to be controlled effectively along the perimeter of the building. The use of an exposed-concrete structure internally assists in reducing temperature fluctuations by storing warmth and coolness within the building frame, reducing peak energy loads.

The building employs a displacement ventilation system, offering a number of benefits in terms of reduced energy use and occupant comfort. The system enables the use of operable windows and passive ventilation in the mid-season periods to supplement the building services systems, as the cooling systems can be shut down and the mechanical ventilation system's fresh-air supply can be supplemented with air that comes in from opening the windows. This strategy delivers major benefits to the tenants by providing user control over the internal environment and enhancing occupant comfort, and it is seen by clients as a major marketing benefit.

The displacement ventilation system employs large volumes of relatively high-temperature fresh air, supplied via a plenum floor at a reduced velocity, thus minimizing the risk of drafts for occupants. |7 The system also ensures that the internal air quality is very good compared with a minimum fresh-air system, which uses the smallest volume

Integrated Building Envelope Strategies   143

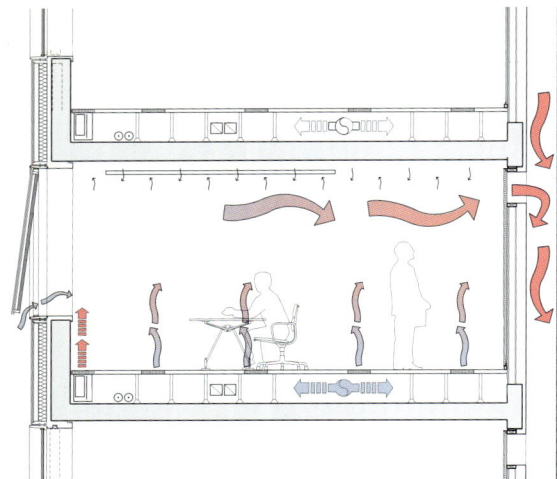

7 | Environmental section diagram: The plenum floor void supplies fresh air, which can be supplemented through the opening of windows. Internal heat gains warm the fresh air, which rises and is then extracted through risers in the core to the basement plant.

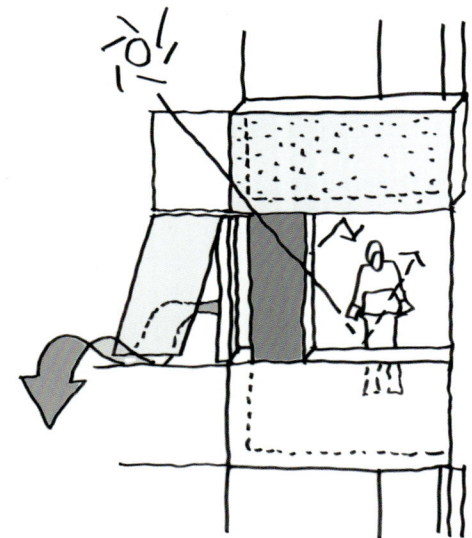

8 | Working sketch showing user contact, operation, and scale of the building envelope

of fresh air necessary to maintain the internal environment and consequently must be supplied with air at a substantially lower temperature. The Charlotte Building's supply-air temperature of 18–19 degrees Celsius (64–66 degrees Fahrenheit) means that during spring and fall in London, air can be supplied without conditioning, effectively eliminating the energy load required for cooling at these times. Providing operable windows, as described previously, allows direct control of the immediate environment and provides access to additional fresh air. This control gives the occupants a greater connection with the outside and reduces the feeling of being "sealed" within the building. |8

The Charlotte Building's low-energy mechanical ventilation system is not intended to deal with large cooling loads, so climate-control demands are partially dealt with by the envelope itself. To do this, it was necessary to limit the amount of clear glass used in the building envelope to limit the effects of solar heat gain, which would otherwise increase operational energy demands. The clear glazed area was reduced to around 40 percent of the envelope's surface, compared with a more conventionally serviced building, where a 60 percent or higher area of clear glass might be possible, but with substantially greater energy costs.

In order to further minimize energy use, the architects used high-performance clear glass (Low-E, argon-filled units to reduce heat transfer) where called for in the building envelope. This required detailed consideration of the extent and location of windows to maximize daylighting and views while controlling solar gain. The use of a solid spandrel up to 750 millimeters (29.5 inches) above finished-floor level reduced the amount of glazing while maximizing views out for occupants from their desks. This placement of glazing also creates a more even distribution of daylight across the space by reducing the illuminance gradient from the perimeter to the

9 Prototype panel detail of column casing and top-hung, outward-opening vent

Integrated Building Envelope Strategies

center of the plan, increasing the perceived level of daylighting internally.

Delivering the End Product
Achieving the correct final result with a bespoke cladding system requires considerable investment in prototyping and testing, not only in terms of technical performance but also with regard to the aesthetic details of the system. A number of mock-ups and full prototypes were produced for the Charlotte Building, from single cladding panels fabricated to test the overall appearance of a typical unit on-site, to small-scale models of the shadow box spandrel elements created to explore the proportions and depth of the units and fritting patterns. |9

10| Testing of the envelope's watertightness

Once the architects and cladding contractor completed the detailed technical design for the typical elements, a full prototype was produced and subjected to rigorous testing in order to prove the performance of the system. This testing regime—based on protocol from the Centre for Window and Cladding Technology (CWCT) in the United Kingdom—involved subjecting the unit to simulated rainfall and wind pressure cycles using a specialized testing rig to ensure watertightness and safety under extreme weather conditions. |10-11 This also allowed the system fabrication, assembly, and installation to be tested before the manufacturing of the final cladding elements began, identifying problems in advance of construction on-site.

11 | A testing rig spraying water on the prototype panel

Achieving "Best Value"
Best value is achieved by using the most appropriate and cost-effective approach that also balances the individual demands of the project—appearance, deliverability, program, performance, and budget—against the client's requirements. For a high-specification project such as the Charlotte Building, where the aim is to achieve a "headquarters"-type

12 | Mock-up panel being lowered into position on site: Constructed by a model maker using MDF, glass, and Perspex, this full-scale model was used to explore the concept design in the very early stages of the project.

project for a speculative market, the building's identity is all-important.

Because of the relatively small size of the project (65,500 square feet), the cladding contractor's design, tooling, and prototyping costs for the facade were proportionately high, and it was of particular importance that the design was efficient and that the number of different components could be minimized. For example, the primary framing systems for holding both the facade's glazing and gold-colored column casings had the same custom extrusion profile.

The overall cost of a facade of this nature is influenced by a diverse range of parameters, many of which have little or no impact on the performance or appearance of the finished system. It is possible to engineer the costs down without impacting quality through consideration of issues such as the production process, workers' handling of components in the factory and on-site, and the amount of material used to produce each element. Value engineering a prefabricated, unitized facade system such as this has much in common with processes in the automotive industry, which is very heavily driven by the fabrication process, waste-avoidance, and production and assembly lines. If savings can be made by using fewer components and materials or installation can be made faster, then these are all engineered into the design to speed up fabrication and assembly. The creation of a custom curtain wall is very similar, in that design decisions early on can have a substantial impact on the speed of fabrication in the factory and on potential cost savings, without altering the appearance or performance of the finished system. This approach enhances the quality of the end product by putting the design and technical performance of the facade system at the forefront of the process.

Notes

Introduction
1. Architecture 2030, United States Energy Information Administration data, http://www.architecture2030.org/.

Section I:
Feedback Loops of Form and Performance
1. Matthias Sauerbruch, "Sustainability, or the Redefinition of the Pleasure Principle," *Harvard Design Magazine* 30 (Spring/Summer 2009): 60-67.

Comfort at the Scale of the Body
1. Assistant Professor Herman Pontzer, Washington University in St. Louis, Department of Anthropology, personal communication with the author, May 27, 2009.
2. Max Fordham, "The Role of Comfort in Happiness," in *Building Happiness: Architecture to Make You Smile,* ed. Jane Wernick (London: Black Dog Publishing Ltd., 2008), 56-65.
3. American Society of Heating, Refrigerating and Air-Conditioning Engineers, Inc. (ASHRAE), *Standard 55-2004–Thermal Environmental Conditions for Human Occupancy (ANSI Approved)* (Atlanta, GA: ASHRAE, 2004). This standard specifies conditions or comfort zones where 80 percent of sedentary or slightly active persons find the environment thermally acceptable.
4. Ibid., 3.
5. Ibid., 1.
6. Michelle Addington and Daniel Schodek, *Smart Materials and Technologies for the Architecture and Design Professions* (Amsterdam and Boston, MA: Architectural Press, 2005).

Climate and Context
1. With reference to Bob Allies and Graham Morrison, "A Particular Point of View," in *MAP (Michigan Architecture Papers) 2: Allies and Morrison* (Ann Arbor, MI: University of Michigan College of Architecture Business Office, 1996).
2. Matthew Herman, Buro Happold Consulting Engineers, personal communication with the author, 2008-9.

Interdisciplinary to Transdisciplinary
1. Anna Dyson, director of the Center for Architecture Science and Ecology and associate professor at the School of Architecture at Rensselaer, personal communication with the author.
2. Basarab Nicolescu, ed., *Transdisciplinarity: Theory and Practice* (Cresskill, NJ: Hampton Press Inc., 2008).
3. Anna Dyson, pers. comm.

Materials and Fabrication
1. With reference to Michelle Addington and Daniel Schodek, *Smart Materials and Technologies for the Architecture and Design Professions* (Amsterdam and Boston, MA: Architectural Press, 2005).
2. Centre for Window and Cladding Technology, "Cladding Metals 1–Ferrous Metals," calculated from Technical Note 22, http://www.cwct.co.uk/publications/tns/short22.pdf.
3. John Fernandez, *Material Architecture: Emergent Materials for Innovative Buildings and Ecological Construction* (Boston, MA: Architectural Press, 2006).
4. Arup engineer Tali Mejicovsky, personal communication with the author, July 31, 2009.
5. Permasteelisa Group, personal communication with the author, May/June 2009.

Life Cycle Analysis
1. Gary Lawrence of Arup, personal communication with the author, August 2007.
2. Stephen Mudie, building envelope specialist and partner at Davis Langdon LLP (a global construction consultancy), personal communication with the author, 2008 and 2009.
3. U.S. Environmental Protection Agency, "Life-Cycle Assessment (LCA)," http://www.epa.gov/ORD/NRMRL/lcaccess/.
4. NIST Handbook 135, "Life-Cycle Costing Manual for the Federal Energy Management Program," 1995 edition, http://www.fire.nist.gov/bfrlpubs/build96/PDF/b96121.pdf.
5. For example, see *Buildings and Constructed Assets: Service-life planning*, "Part 5: Life-Cycle Costing" (International Organization for Standards, 2008), http://www.iso.org/iso/catalogue_detail.htm?csnumber=29430.
6. Stanford University Land and Buildings, "Guidelines for Life Cycle Analysis," October 2005, http://lbre.stanford.edu/dpm/sites/all/lbre-shared/files/docs_public/LCCA121405.pdf.
7. Center for Building Performance and Diagnostics, Carnegie Mellon University School of Architecture, "Building Investment Decision Support," http://cbpd.arc.cmu.edu/bidstrial/pages/home.aspx http://cbpd.arc.cmu.edu/bidstrial/pages/intro.aspx?id=5.

Section II:
Elements of a Holistic Approach
1. Patrick Bellew, building services engineer and founding director at Atelier Ten, London, personal communication with the author, May 2009.

Air: Flow and Ventilation
1. SBS complaints may be localized in a particular room or zone, or be widespread throughout a building. In contrast, the term "building-related illness" (BRI) is used when symptoms of diagnosable illness are identified and can be attributed directly to airborne building contaminants. The Environmental Protection Agency's definition of SBS can be found at http://www.epa.gov/iaq/pubs/sbs.html.
2. Center for the Built Environment, "About Mixed Mode," http://www.cbe.berkeley.edu/mixedmode/aboutmm.html.
3. CASE team members for the APS project: Anna Dyson, director of research and principal investigator (PI); Ted Ngai, architectural design and Co-PI; Jason Vollen, manufacturing design and Co-PI; Lupita Montoya, mechanical engineering and Co-PI; Paul Mankiewicz, biologist and Co-PI; Miki Amitay, mechanical engineering; Ahu Aydogan, architecture PhD candidate; Michael Paul Allard, mechanical engineering PhD candidate; EmilyRae Brayton, architectural researcher.

Heat: Gain and Loss

1. Patrick Bellew at Atelier Ten, personal communication with the author.
2. Advanced EcoCeramic Envelope Systems are in advanced development at the Center for Architecture Science and Ecology (CASE) at Rensselaer Polytechnic Institute by Jason Vollen, associate professor and director of research; and Kelly Winn, architecture PhD candidate. Through the University of Arizona's (UA) Emerging Material Technologies Graduate Program, Jed Laver, a UA master's student, materially contributed to the research. Advisors include Professor Álvaro Malo from UA and Dale Clifford from CMU.

Water: Systems and Collection

1. Christopher Kloss, "Managing Wet Weather with Green Infrastructure Municipal Handbook: Rainwater Harvesting Policies" (Environmental Protection Agency, Dec. 2008), http://www.epa.gov/npdes/pubs/gi_munichandbook_harvesting.pdf.
2. Water Encyclopedia, http://www.weatherexplained.com/Vol-1/Air-and-Water-Pollution.html.
3. National Institute of Building Sciences, *Whole Building Design Guide*, "Building Envelope Design Guide–Curtain Walls," http://www.wbdg.org/design/env_fenestration_cw.php#funda.
4. Kloss, "Managing Wet Weather with Green Infrastructure Municipal Handbook: Rainwater Harvesting Policies."
5. American Society of Heating, Refrigerating and Air-Conditioning Engineers (ASHRAE), "ASHRAE GreenTip #37: Rainwater Harvesting," in *ASHRAE GreenGuide*, 2nd edition (Atlanta, GA: ASHRAE, 2006), 312.
6. United Kingdom House of Commons, "Flood and Water Management Bill–Draft," April 21, 2009. This draft legislation in the United Kingdom aims to increase the use of sustainable drainage systems (SUDS) by ending the automatic right to connect to sewers for surface water drainage and demanding that developers put SUDS into place in new developments "wherever practicable." It is expected to become law in 2011. See http://www.defra.gov.uk/environment/water/strategy/pdf/future-water.pdf.
7. The Solar Building Envelope is being developed at the Center for Architecture Science and Ecology (CASE) at Rensselaer Polytechnic Institute by Jason Vollen, architecture co-principal investigator (Co-PI); Anna Dyson, architecture Co-PI; Dr. Peter Stark, physicist; and Kristin Malone, architecture PhD Candidate.

Materials: Assemblies and Installation

1. Michelle Addington and Daniel Schodek, *Smart Materials and Technologies for the Architecture and Design Professions* (Amsterdam and Boston, MA: Architectural Press, 2005).
2. National Institute of Building Sciences, *Whole Building Design Guide*, "Building Envelope Design Guide–Curtain Walls," http://www.wbdg.org/design/env_fenestration_cw.php#funda.
3. Pilkington North Amercia Inc. technical department, telephone conversation with author, September 2009.
4. Roberto Bicchiarelli of Permasteelisa Group, personal communication with the author.
5. Ian Ferguson, *Buildability in Practice* (London: Batsford, 1989), 9.
6. PCM team: Professor Paul J. Donnelly, Washington University in St. Louis; Professor Ramesh Agarwal, Washington University in St. Louis; Professor Rachel Becker, Technion–Israel Institute of Technology's National Building Research Institute; Donald Fedorko, HOK St. Louis; and Troy Fosler, Washington University in St. Louis.
7. Research into structural materials fabricated from post-agricultural waste by-products has been conducted within the Built Ecologies Graduate Program at the Center for Architecture Science and Ecology (CASE) at Rensselaer Polytechnic Institute by the following: Anna Dyson, co-principal investigator (Co-PI); Jason Vollen, Co-PI; Anu Akkineni, PhD student.

Daylighting: Comfort and Control

1. William M. C. Lam, "Environmental Objectives and Human Needs," in *Perception and Lighting as Formgivers for Architecture,* ed. Christopher Hugh Ripman (New York, NY: McGraw-Hill, 1997).
2. Comfort and Low Energy Architecture (CLEAR), "Daylight Factors," www.learn.londonmet.ac.uk/packages/clear/visual/daylight/analysis/hand/daylight_factor.html.
3. Building Energy Codes Resource Center, "What is a Window SHGC?" http://resourcecenter.pnl.gov/cocoon/morf/ResourceCenter/article//93.
4. Lam, "Environmental Objectives and Human Needs."
5. Joel Loveland, "Daylight by Design," *LD + A* (Oct. 2003): 44-48.
6. Chuck Hoberman, "The Art and Science of Folding Structures: New Geometries of Continuous Multidimensional Transformations," in *SITES Architecture* 24, ed. Dennis Dollens. (New York, NY: Lumen, Inc.): 34-53.

Energy: Minimizing and Maximizing

1. Architecture 2030, U.S. Energy Information Administration data, http://www.architecture2030.org/current_situation/building_sector.html.
2. Michelle Addington, "No Building Is an Island: A Look at the Different Scales of Energy," *Harvard Design Magazine* 26 (Spring/Summer 2007): 38-45.
3. U.S. Energy Information Administration, Office of Energy Markets and End Use, 2001 Residential Energy Consumption Survey, http://www.eia.doe.gov/emeu/recs/recs2001/enduse2001/enduse2001.html.
4. Royal Institute of British Architects (RIBA), "Carbon Literacy Briefing," http://www.architecture.com/FindOutAbout/Sustainabilityandclimatechange/ClimateChange/CarbonLiteracyBriefing.aspx.
5. Architecture 2030, "Measures of Sustainability," http://www.canadianarchitect.com/asf/perspectives_sustainibility/measures_of_sustainablity/measures_of_sustainablity_embodied.htm.
6. Ibid.
7. U.S. Department of Energy, "Building Sector Expenditures," http://buildingsdatabook.eren.doe.gov/TableView.aspx?table=1.2.3. This table relates to cost, not consumption.
8. Joel Loveland, "Daylight by Design," *LD + A* (Oct. 2003): 44-48.
9. Comfort and Low Energy Architecture (CLEAR), "Daylighting and Visual Comfort," http://www.learn.londonmet.ac.uk/packages/clear/index.html.
10. Dr. Raymond Cole, professor at the School of Architecture and

Landscape architecture at the University of British Columbia, keynote lecture at the Passive and Low Energy Architecture (PLEA) conference, June 22-24, 2009.

11 Kathryn Janda ,"Buildings Don't Use Energy; People Do," in *Architecture, Energy, and the Occupant's Perspective*, Passive Low Energy Architecture (PLEA) 2009 conference proceedings, ed. Claude Demers and André Potvin.

12 The Integrated Concentrating system is being developed in the Center for Architecture Science and Ecology (CASE) at Rensselaer Polytechnic Institute by Anna Dyson, director of research and principal investigator (PI); Michael Jensen, mechanical engineering; Kyle Brooks and Steven Derby, mechanical engineering and robotics; Jesse Craft, mechanical engineering; Joshua Emig, architecture; Tim Eliassen, structural engineering; Skye Gruen, environmental engineering PhD candidate; Ryan Salvas, architecture graduate student.

Section III:
Integrated Building Envelope Strategies

Deep Plan

1 *Arup Newsletter* 16 (Oct. 1963): 28-29.
2 Herbert Girardet, "Sustaining Design," in *Arup Associates: Unified Design*, ed. Paul Brislin (London: John Wiley & Sons, 2008), 54.
3 Paul Brislin, personal communication with the author.

Feedback Loops

1 Buro Happold, project team document at RIBA Stage D.
2 Ibid.
3 Geun Young Yun and Koen Steemers, "Time-dependent occupant behaviour models of window control in summer," *Building and Environment* 43, no. 9 (2008): 1471-82. See also Geun Young Yun, Koen Steemers, and Nick Baker, "Natural ventilation in practice: Building design, occupant behaviour and thermal performance," *Building Research & Information* 36, no. 6 (2008): 608-24.
4 Gavin Stamp, "Taming the zoo," *Building Design* (Oct. 8, 2004), http://www.bdonline.co.uk/story.asp?storycode=3041744.

Bibliography

1. Printed Sources

Addington, Michelle D., and Daniel Schodek. *Smart Materials and New Technologies: for the Architecture and Design Professions*. Amsterdam, NETH, and Boston, MA: Architectural Press, 2005.

American Society of Heating, Refrigerating and Air-Conditioning Engineers, Inc. *ASHRAE GreenGuide: The Design, Construction, and Operation of Sustainable Buildings*. Atlanta, GA: ASHRAE, 2006.

———. "ASHRAE Technical Committees." 2nd ed. *ASHRAE GreenGuide*. Atlanta, GA: ASHRAE, 2006.

———. *Thermal Environmental Conditions for Human Occupancy*. Atlanta, GA: ASHRAE, 2004.

Asimakopoulos, D. N. *Energy and Climate in the Urban Built Environment*. Edited by Mat Santanmouris. London, UK: James & James, 2001.

Banham, Reyner. *The Architecture of the Well-Tempered Environment*. 2nd ed. Chicago, IL: University of Chicago Press, 1984.

British Council for Offices. *2009 Guide to Specification*. London, UK: British Council for Offices, 2009.

Brock, Linda. *Designing the Exterior Wall: an Architectural Guide to the VerticalEnvelope*. Hoboken, NJ: Wiley, 2005.

Brown, G. Z. *Sun, Wind & Light: Architectural Design Strategies*. 2nd ed. New York, NY: Wiley, 2001.

Burroughs, William, ed. *Climate: Into the 21st Century*. Cambridge, UK: Cambridge University Press, 2003.

Clarke, Joseph. *Energy Simulation in Building Design*. 2nd ed. Oxford, UK: Butterworth-Heinemann, 2001.

Daniels, Klaus. *The Technology of Ecological Building: Basic Principles and Measures, Examples and Ideas*. Translated by Elizabether Schwaiger. Basel, SWI: Birkhäuser, 1997.

Demkin, Joseph A., ed. *The Architect's Handbook of Professional Practice*. 14th ed. Hoboken, NJ: Wiley, 2008.

Fernandez, John. *Material Architecture: Emergent Materials for Innovative Buildings and Ecological Construction*. Boston, MA: Architectural Press, 2006.

Fitch, James Marston. *American Building: The Environmental Forces That Shape It*. Oxford, UK: Oxford University Press, 1999.

Hegger, Manfred. *Energy Manual: Sustainable Architecture*. Translated by Gerd H. Söffker, Philip Thrift, and Pamela Seidel. Basel, SWI: Birkhäuser, 2008.

Herzog, Thomas, Roland Krippner, and Werner Lang. *Façade Construction Manual*. Basel, SWI: Birkhäuser, 2004.

Hunt, William Dudley. *The Contemporary Curtain Wall: Its Design, Fabrication and Erection*. New York, NY: F.W. Dodge, 1958.

Ken, Yeang. *Ecodesign: A Manual for Ecological Design*. London, UK: Wiley, 2006.

Larson, Greg Ward, and Rob Shakespeare. *Rendering with Radiance: The Art and Science of Lighting Visualization*. San Francisco, CA: Morgan Kauffman, 1998.

Lechner, Norbert. *Heating, Cooling, Lighting: Design Methods for Architects*. New York, NY: Wiley, 1991.

Case Study Project Credits

Adelaide Wharf Housing
Client: First Base Ltd. and English Partnerships
Architect: Allford Hall Monaghan Morris LLP Architects
Structural engineer: Adams Kara Taylor
Environmental engineer: Waterman Building Services
Quantity surveyor: Faithful + Gould
Main contractor: Bovis Lend Lease
Cladding contractor: Sipral
Key dates:
   Start of construction: April 2006
   Completion: October 2007

160 Tooley Street Offices
Client: Great Portland Estates plc
Architect: Allford Hall Monaghan Morris LLP Architects
Structural engineer: Arup
Environmental engineer: Arup
Quantity surveyor: Gardiner & Theobald LLP
Main contractor: Laing O'Rourke
Cladding contractor: Schneider (unitized system); Mallings (precast concrete)
Key dates:
   Start of construction: 2004
   Completion: June 2008

Harlequin 1, BSkyB Transmission and Recording Facility
Client: British Sky Broadcasting Ltd. (BSkyB) and Stanhope plc
Architect: Arup Associates
Structural engineer: Arup Associates
Environmental engineer: Arup Associates
Quantity surveyor: Davis Langdon LLP
Main contractor: Bovis Lend Lease
Cladding contractor: Lindner Schmidlin
Key dates:
   Start of construction: November 2007
   Completion (shell and core/fitout): February 2010
   Completion (technical fitout): November 2011

Faculty of English and Institute of Criminology
Client: Estate Management and Building Service (EMBS), University of Cambridge
Architect: Allies and Morrison
Structural engineer: WhitbyBird Engineers
Environmental engineer: Buro Happold
Quantity surveyor: Faithful + Gould
Main contractor: Wates Group
Cladding contractor: Schneider
Key dates:
   Master plan commissioned: 2000
   Start of construction: 2002
   Building occupation: 2004
   Post-occupancy evaluation: 2008

Tooley Street Terrace
Client: More London Development
Architect: Hawkins\Brown
Structural engineer: Adams Kara Taylor
Environmental engineer: RHB Partnership LLP
Cost consultant: EC Harris
Contractor: Haymills (Contractors) Ltd.
Cladding contractor: Fleetwood Architectural Aluminium
Key dates:
   Start of construction: Spring 2007
   Building occupation: Summer 2008

290 Mulberry Street
Client: Cardinal Real Estate Investments
Architect: SHoP Architects
Structural engineer: Robert Silman Associates
Environmental engineer: Laszlo Bodak Engineer P.C.
Main contractor: Kiska Group Ltd.
Panel fabricator: Saramac
Liner fabricator: Architectural Polymers
Key dates:
   Start of construction: 2007
   Expected completion: 2009

The Charlotte Building
Client: Derwent London plc
Architect: Lifschutz Davidson Sandilands
Structural engineer: Adams Kara Taylor
Environmental engineer: Norman Disney & Young
Quantity surveyor/project manager: Jackson Coles
Main contractor: Balfour Beatty Construction Scottish and Southern Ltd.
Cladding contractor: Fahrni Facade Systems AG
Key dates:
   Start of construction: July 2007
   Completion: October 2009

Major, Mark, Jonathan Speirs, and Anthony Tischhauser. *Made of Light: The Art of Light and Architecture*. Basel, SWI: Birkhäuser, 2004.

Malkawi, Ali M. and Godfried Augenbroe, eds. *Advanced Building Simulation*. New York, NY: Spoon Press, 2003.

McEvoy, Michael. *External Components*. 4th ed. Mitchell's Building Series. Harlow, UK: Longman, 1994.

Olesen, B. W. and G. S. Brager. "A Better Way to Predict Comfort: The New ASHRAE Standard 55-2004." *ASHRAE Journal*. 20-26, 2004.

Santamouris, Mat and Dejan Mumovic, eds. *A Handbook of Sustainable Building Design and Engineering: an Integrated Approach to Energy, Health, and Operational Performance*. London, UK: Earthscan, 2009.

Schittich, Christian, ed. *In Detail: Building Skins: Concepts, Layers, Materials*. Basel, SWI: Birkhäuser, 2001.

Silver, Pete, and Will McLean. *Introduction to Architectural Technology*. London, UK: Laurence King Publishing, 2008.

Smith, Jacqueline, ed. *The Facts on File Dictionary of Weather and Climate*. New York, NY: Facts on File, 2006.

Smith, Peter F. *Architecture in a Climate of Change: A Guide to Sustainable Design*. Boston, MA: Architectural Press, 2001.

Stein, Benjamin and John S. Reynolds. *Mechanical and Electrical Equipment for Buildings*. 9th ed. New York, NY: Wiley, 2005.

Szokolay, Steven V. *Introduction to Architectural Science: The Basis of Sustainable Design*. Boston, MA: Architectural Press, 2004.

Tochihara, Yutaka and Tadakatsu Ohnaka. *Environmental Ergonomics: The Ergonomics of Human Comfort, Health, and Performance in the Thermal Environment*. Amsterdam, NETH: Elsevier, 2005.

Watts, Andrew. *Modern Construction Facades*. New York, NY: Springer, 2005.

———. *Modern Construction Handbook*. New York, NY: Springer, 2001.

Wigginton, Michael and Jude Harris. *Intelligent Skins*. Oxford, UK: Butterworth-Heinemann, 2002.

2. Internet Sources

American Society of Heating, Refrigerating and Air-Conditioning Engineers, Inc.

"ASHRAE Technical Committee 2.1–Physiology and Human Environment: Frequently Asked Questions." http://tc21.ashraetcs.org /faq.html.

Autodesk. "TheWeather Tool." Autodesk Ecotect. http://ecotect.com/products/weathertool.

Bazjanac, Vladimir. "Building Information Modeling for the e-Lab at LBNL." Lawrence Berkley National Laboratory. http://bim.arch.gatech.edu/data /reference/elab.pdf.

Briggs, Robert S., Robert G. Lucas, and Z. Todd Taylor. "Climate Classification for Building Energy Codes and Standards." http://www.energycodes.gov/implement/pdfs/climate_paper_review_draft_rev.pdf.

Building Enclosure Council. "Whole Building Design Guide." Building Envelope Design Guide. http://www.wbdg.org/design/envelope.php.

Building Sustainable Design. "CPD Module 6: Comfort for Productivity in Offices." Building Services Journal. http://www.bsdlive.co.uk/story.asp?storycode=3068212.

Cheung, K.P. "The Sun and Building Design Process, I & II." http://www.arch.hku.hk/teaching/lecture/65156-8.htm.

"Climates of the World." Climate Zone. http://www.climate-zone.com/.

Department of Environmental Health Faculty of Health Science. "Solar Energy: From Earth to the Sun." Solar Disinfection of Drinking Water and Oral Rehydration Solutions: Guidelines for Household Application in Developing Countries. http://almashriq.hiof.no/lebanon/600/610/614/solar-water/unesco/21-23.html.

"Energy Code Climate Zones." Building Energy Codes Resource Center. http://resourcecenter.pnl.gov/cocoon/morf/ResourceCenter/article//1420.articletopdf?homepage_url=http://resourcecenter.pnl.gov/cocoon/morf/ResourceCenter&site_name=ResourceCenter.

Health and Safety Executive. "What is Thermal Comfort?" http://www.hse.gov.uk/temperature/thermal/explained.htm.

"Rainwater Harvesting Policies." Managing Wet Weather with Green Municipal Handbook: Funding Options. http://www.epa.gov/npdes/pubs/gi_munichandbook_funding.pdf.

Taylor, Todd Z. "New Climate Zones in the IECC 2004 Supplement and ASHRAE Standard 90.1-2004." Paper presented at the 2005 National Workshop Building Energy Codes Program, June 28, 2005. http://www.energycodes.gov/news/2005_workshop/presentations/plenary-day/hot-topics/commercial/t_taylor-new_climate_zones.pdf

U.S. Department of Agriculture. "Wind Rose Data." Natural Resources Conservation Service. http://www.wcc.nrcs.usda.gov/climate/windrose.html.

U.S. Department of Energy: Energy Efficiency and Renewable Energy. "Climate Consultant." Building Energy Software Tools Directory. http://apps1.eere.energy.gov/buildings/tools_directory/software.cfm/ID=123/pagename=alpha_list.

U.S. Department of Energy: Energy Efficiency and Renewable Energy. "Weather Data Sources." EnergyPlus Energy Simulation Software. http://apps1.eere.energy.gov/buildings/energyplus/weatherdata_sources.cfm.

U.S. Department of Energy: Energy Efficiency and Renewable Energy. "Weather Tool." Building Energy Software Tools Directory. http://apps1.eere.energy.gov/buildings/tools_directory/software.cfm/ID=375/pagename=alpha_list.

"Weather and Climate Change." Met Office. http://www.metoffice.gov.uk/.

World Climates. http://www.blueplanetbiomes.org/climate.htm.